I0167826

LAO TZU ☯ QIGONG

KENICHI SHIODA

1ˢᵗ Edition

SouthLetters

LAO TZU ☯ QIGONG

Includes Bibliographical references and Index

ISBN:
978-1-943350-27-8

4

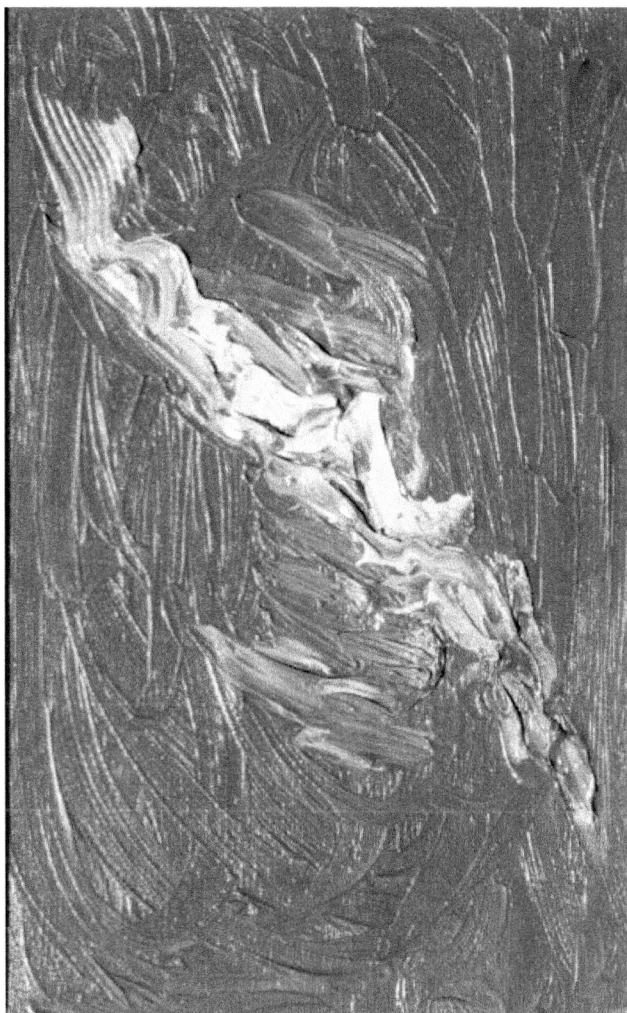

In full stillness I glimpsed the sublime
Yang Xiàn Tzu

CONTENT

Translation

Extension project 'Tradutório' - Modern Languages Department

UNESP Assis. São Paulo, Brazil

Dra. Regiani A. S. Zacarias (coord.)

Fabrício Leal Bernardo

Isadora Lapetina Moran

Jéssica da Cruz Ferreira

Júlia de Camargo Schaefer

Vivian Nádia Ribeiro de Moraes

Renan de Oliveira Camargo Andrada

Review and Organization

Dra. Cecília Kimie Jo Shioda

Dra. Regiani A. S. Zacarias

PREFACE

The title of this book is "Lao Tzu ☯ Qigong", in order to make the reader understand the *Tao Te Ching* (The Book of the Path and the Virtue) by Qigong.

It is very important to observe that the original book was written in Japanese, and that the work of translation does not simply mean to find an equivalent word in another language, but to contextualize by studying some texts and articles on the topic, published in English must be taken into consideration. Therefore, this translation does not strictly follow the original Japanese version but focuses on the cohesion and coherence of the English text, on the precise understanding of the subject, and especially on Master Shioda's interpretation of, "The Book of the Path and the Virtue".

All poems are permeated by my interpretation, not containing literal translation.

Qigong is a technique to introduce, in our body, the *Chi* that exists in nature, in the Great universe. Its ultimate objective is to capture the postnatal Energy (this definition will be better explained throughout the book) and eliminate the diseases of our body (called Small Universe).

Even today, many leading figures estudied the *Tao Te Ching* of the great Master Lao Tzu, but none of them explains the method called *Senshū Kōhō* 仙修功法, which is the learning through Taoist practices performed by the *sennin* (mountain wizards or monks).

Another important issue is the ideograms, or *kanji*, conceived over 10,000 years ago by the ancient Taoists. The pictographic *kanji* has already been explained by linguists of today. Wavy lines ⦀, for example, conceived from the *kanji* "kawa" (川 /kawa/ = river) means looking at the water flowing from the mountain. However, there are many abstract ideograms, such as *"Chi"*, which means Energy. Only by interpreting the meaning of abstract ideograms, one is able to understand the book of Lao Tzu.

The Master Shioda's philosophy about abstract ideograms, as well as the internal and external practices of Qigong have been included in this book in order to improve the reader's understanding.

An important question is why did the great Master Lao Tzu not leave *Senshū Kōhō* in a book format, as he did with his poems? Since ancient times *Senshū Kōhō* has been transmitted orally [only for people who have the 'kei'], and this has kept it from being disseminated worldwide.

Master *Liu Pai Lin* was born in the early twentieth century in Tietsin, People's Republic of China. He began his studies of Taoism from an early age, by assimilating different styles (Dragon Gate - *Lón Mén*, Golden Mountain - *Jīn Shān*, Mountain of China - *Kún Lún*, Blue Castle - *Qīng Chéng*, Floating Hill - *Fú Qiū*). At the same time, he joined the Army and retired as lieutenant general of his division. Until the day of his death, at the age of 92, on February 2, 2000, he devoted himself to the arts of Taoism, Tai Chi Chuan and *Bāguàzhǎng* with great vitality. He assisted his patients until four hours before his death. He also made public the secret compilation of the "Taoist Qigong".

At that time, he disseminated Taoism teachings in different countries such as China, Taiwan, Japan, Brazil, Argentina, Mexico, Portugal and the U.S.A.

This book is a compendium of Master Liu Pai Lin's teachings, and we might say it is a work of co-authorship. Although there was this plan of translating this book into each and every language on Earth, as I was writing it I added some thoughts about Taoism in order contribute to a better understanding.

Is it possible for these teachings to be suppressed in 100, 200, 500 years? Tao (Path) is a teaching about nature. "God" is nature. Consequently, Tao is God. There is nothing in this world that surpasses the teachings and the Divinity of Tao.

To write the originals of this work, Master Shioda has had the help and guidance of Master Tanigawa, Master Yoshitsugu Hayashi and of the son of Master Liu Pai Lin, Liu Chih Ming. "My companion of Taoism, Yuzo Higuchi (professor emeritus at the National University of Technology,

Tokyo) who was kind enough to revise the text". For editing the original book, Master Shioda had the collaboration of Mr. Toshio Hirota on both the proofreading and graphic services.

I would also like to record sincere appreciation and gratitude to:

- Mr. Akinori Kajisako, photographer;

- Mrs. Eliana Sant'Anna Menegaldo de Camargo, our beloved disciple, who made a thorough review and served as a photographic model;

- Mr. Kazuhide Sainowaki, ex-director of an important publishing house, who contributed with valuable advices;

- Those who made important contributions to the production, the disciple John, Dr.Cecilia Kimie Shioda, Dr. Regiani Zacarias, Fabrício Leal Bernardo, Isadora Lapetina Moran, Jéssica da Cruz Ferreira, Júlia de Camargo Schaefer, Vivian Nádia Ribeiro de Moraes, Renan de Oliveira Camargo Andrada e Renato da Fonseca Brandão, as well as many other collaborators.

Explanatory Notes[1]

About the objective of this book

To serve as source for those who want to learn about health and longevity.

To be a basic reading for those who wish to venture into the first path of Taoism.

To disseminate Taoism, serving as a reference book and transmitting the secrets of *Qigong* to those who aim to become masters.

About the book

It consists of 5 chapters and 10 sub-chapters.

Composition of the 5 chapters: history of Taoism, health and longevity, the teachings of the *Tao Te Ching* (The Book of the Path and the Virtue) of the great Master Lao Tzu, illustrated manual with techniques and Taoist practices for capturing energy, specific treatment practice of *Qigong*.

Orthography and vocabulary

For phonetic transcriptions of some ideograms, the universally known spelling was adopted. And about the vocabulary, contemporary terms were used in order to facilitate the understanding of readers.

---

1 When we decided to translate the original original book in Japanese into English soon after the Portuguese edition was published, we found ourselves facing a huge challenge due to the obstacles associated to the distance between these languages, and to the fact that only one person in the translation group spoke Japanese. One of the solutions was to translate from the Portuguese version and to ask the author for explanations whenever it was possible. Another solution was to do a vast research on published articles about the topic, create a glossary and schedule regular meetings to discuss and decide the final English text.

Photographs and DVD

The photographs were taken at the Shioda Center of Health, during the *Qigong* morning exercises practiced by the author and his student Eliana.

The photos and DVD (Sold separately on Amazon) serve as support and guidance for the practices.

Our intention, with the photos and DVD, is to demonstrate how to effectively lead the essence of *Qigong*. In addition to the annexes to *Naikikō* practice (internal *Qigong*) and *Gaikikō* (external *Qigong*), new to the public, exercises for capturing Energy, Tao Gymnastics, Tai Chi Chuan and *Bāguàzhăng* Pai Lin style for a healthy life are also included.

For those who aim for longevity and health, the energy practices in this DVD should be done daily and should be seen not as a morning obligation, but as a moment of pleasure or self-knowledge.

Taoist Masters

Master Tai Lai Sun

Master Nan Shu

Master Liu Pai Lin

Master Lyao Kun

18

1. The Birth of Lao Tzu

According to Taoist teachings transmitted to the present day, the Great Master Lao Tzu was born in the Chinese city of Guo Yang, in the Na Hue province, more precisely at the time of the Rabbit (between five and seven o'clock in the morning) on February 15, 571 B.C. It is said that he lived until about 180 years of age,but the date of his death is not exactly known. Since he is a *sennin* (the name given to a wise man who inhabits the hills after attaining enlightenment), it is quite likely that his death took place in the mountains.

His real name was Li Er, according to Chinese customs, it was common to give a nickname to the boys who reached adulthood; for him, the name was Tan. His best-known name, Lao Tzu, means *old* or *grand (great) master.* He was a great thinker and philosopher of naturalistic tendencies, whose most notable disciple, Chuang Tzu, became famous for making his teachings well-known.

We can presume that Buddha Shakyamuni, the founder of Buddhism, was born 14 years after Lao Tzu in 557 BC, received strong influence from Lao Tzu, as there are many similar sermons from both of them. Taoists believe that Confucius, the founder of Confucianism and born in 551 BC, may also have received teachings and influence of the great master.

A Taoist is, in a few words, a master of nature. They are people who study the laws of nature by joining to the sky and earth, and by introducing in their own bodies the "*Chi*" (Energy) wich emanates from the universe and by expelling the "*Xié*" (disease, illness) to preserve health and longevity. They are the ones who conquer virtue or wisdom through the elevation of the mind - the ultimate objective that guides Taoism.

By learning more about *Tao* (Path), *Toku* (Virtue) and by receiving love, one should instruct the new learners to transmit that same love. This is the second most important objective. Fail to do so and Taoism becomes extinct, because only those that have respect and love within themselves are qualified to be disciples, while those who do not guide them well can never conquer the virtue or wisdom.

醫拳仙修煉秘訣

(*I-Ken-Sen-Shū-Ren-Hi-Ketsu* – Japanese)

(*Yī Quán Xiān Xiū Liàn Mì Jué* – Chinese)

I, 醫 » The cure for the disease. It means to expel the evil Energy. It is a person who cures disease.

KEN, 拳 » It is the state of sincere respect. It means to be respectful and humble. It means having good manners and being modest.

SEN, 仙 » The left side of the ideogram, 亻 represents the man. The right side, 山, represents the mountain. It means "a man who lives in the mountain".

The perfect dwelling for an ascetic is the cave located in the middle of a mountain slope, where there is harmony between the positive and negative energies, near the river with five colored stones. This is one of the secrets of Taoism.

SHŪ, 修» It is the improvement of the soul and body. It means to improve and balance the Yin-Yang correctly.

REN, 煉» It is the training. The left side of this ideogram, training (煉), is fire (火). The fire represents "Positive Energy". With *REN* (煉) the balance between Yin-Yang is improved.

HI, 秘 » Represents the secret and its transmission. It cannot be measured by human wisdom.

KETSU, 訣» It is the arcane sense, a good method.

By living in accordance with Tao (Path) and by treating the Cosmos and Nature in a disciplined manner with gratitude, one can absorb *Chi* (Energy) and expel *Xié* (disease, illness). After a certain period of training, it is possible to penetrate into the "mountain", becoming a "mountain dweller". By submitting to the secret practice of Qigong and devoting oneself to the exercises to enhance spirituality, one can reach the peak of Taoism - good health and longevity. By being devoted to continuous training, anyone can become a wise and virtuous person.

3. THE HISTORY OF TAOISM

Taoism has been transmitted orally since ancient times: its diffusion began about six thousand nine hundred years ago. A Taoist Master saw a white horse with huge black spots. Suddenly, because of this vision, he was enlightened by the perception that black represents Yin and white represents Yang; this way, the theory of Yin-Yang appeared.

The book *Huáng Ting Jīng* (Medical Classic of the Yellow Emperor), discovered in the ruins of a castle nearly 4785 years ago, did not indicate the author's name, but it contained numerous references to techniques for assimilation of *Chi* (Energy). After its publication, in 258 AD, it became a reference for internal Qigong and Taoist studies, and the secrets of this art were deepen around three thousand years ago. At the time, the great master Lao Tzu appeared. In the history of Taoism, there is no record of any previous name to it; therefore,he is considered the first great master, and his work, "The Book of the Path and the Virtue", is unsurpassed, which is why Taoists and religious men took it as their holy book. Later, there was 张紫 陽 *Zhān Zǐ Yáng*, a master who was born in 206 B.C. and died in 200 A.D. (at the age of 406). Among the *Senshū* Taoist lineage he is a well-known professor, who also left immortal poems.

In the early Christian era, master 鼓 祖 *Gǔ Zǔ* was born. Although the general public does not believe it, the Taoists consider that he lived to be 800 years old, approximately. He is known as the longest living Taoist ever. Around the year 1200, master 邱長春 *Chiū Chang Chūn* was born. At that time, in Mongolia, Genghis Khan – who was also born there – one day, invited the Master and asked him: "What is the secret to a long life?" The master replied: "There is no food that will ensure longevity, but there is another way to have a long life." It is a famous episode that points to *Qigong* as the only way to achieve longevity, a truth which applies both to ancient times and today.

Since then branches of Taoism emerged, such as the schools *Lón Mén* (Dragon Gate), *Kún Lún* (Holy Mountain), *Jīn Shān* (Gold Mountain), *Qīng Chéng* (Floating Hill) etc. Master *Chiū Chang Chūn* is the founder of *Lón Mén* Taoism. The tenth supreme master was 了 空*Liao Kōng*, the eleventh was Liu Pai Lin, and the twelfth position is occupied by three masters:

Master Liu Chih Ming, Yoshitsugu Hayashi and Master Kenichi Shioda. Master Liu Pai Lin was a dedicated scholar who received guidance from all Taoist schools, becoming the successor of all. That is, the fifth successor of the *Jīn Shān* School and fourteenth successor of the *Kún Lún*. Therefore, the last three, his direct disciples, became disciples of all of them, and all those dedicated to Taoism are currently receiving excellent technical guidance from all schools combined.

Besides the teachers aforementioned, there are two others that also deserve to be named: Master 张三峰 *Zhān Sān Fēng* (1279 - 1368, 89 years old), famous creator of Tai Chi Chuan; and master 薰 海川 *Xūn Hǎ Chuan*, creator of *Bāguàzhǎng* (1797 - 1882), who stood out for his work and contributions. The teachings of both are being released worldwide as part of dynamic *Qigong* 動(氣)功. For the good of all humankind, the Taoist has, as his sacred mission, the orientation of the static (靜功) and the dynamic (動功) *Qigong*, developing them, spreading them and forming disciples

4. Senshū Kōhō Exercises and Practices

We call *Senshu Koho* the Qigong exercises and practices which are executed with the introduction of *Chi* (Energy) captured from nature or from the Universe in order to become an enlightened master. The objective is to increase spirituality, prevent diseases and maintain good health and longevity.

Senshū Kōhō is usually known by the names: *Naikikō* (internal) or *Naiyōkō* (internal cure) and *Gaikikō* (external) ou *Gaiki Iryō Kōhō* (external therapy). However, among those who search for enlightenment, there are not many who practice the latter, perhaps because when they do not raise the level of *Naikikō* (internal), they lose *Zhen Chi* (prenatal Energy).

The practice of *Qigong* allows the prevention and treatment of various diseases considered fatal by Western medicine. There is no better remedy.

Chi or Energy

It is divided into two groups: *pre* and *postnatal* energy.

Prenatal Energy

Prenatal Energy is the fruit of the union between man's Yin (father) and woman's Yang (mother). That union creates the "child". The child's innate *Chi* is known as "prenatal energy."

Post-natal Energy

It is the energy of the universe that is captured by means of specific processes and techniques, stored in the "navel" (*Tāi Yuán Xué* - Tai Chi Ball) and distributed throughout the body.

For a better understanding, imagine a bank where the money that is deposited is the "Prenatal Energy". The money earned from work is the "Post-natal energy". As much as possible, one preserves the Prenatal Energy carefully, and by depositing the Post-natal energy, one lives a peaceful life. The "Prenatal Energy" may reduce, but never increase. For this reason, it is necessary to deposit "Post-natal Energy" daily, like the food that is consumed every day.

Generally, people use the "Prenatal Energy" without obtaining "Post-natal Energy" and die around the age of 80. The enlightened masters capture "Post-natal Energy" daily, so there are many cases of Taoists who lived for over 130 years. Even with the advancement of modern medicine, the common person will find difficulty to exceed 120 years of age with good physical and mental health.

The enlightened masters introduce the *Chi* into the pituitary gland (hypophysis) daily, activating the brain, the cerebellum and the cranial nerves, achieving longevity with full lucidity until their last days. With no diseases (ilnesses), they do not suffer. They await Tao (deity) to continue their journey into a higher world, where the *Chi* is extinguished.

Naikikō

The *Naikikō,* also known as *Naiyoko* (internal healing *Qigong*) or *Hoken Kiko* (preventive health), is subdivided into two groups:

(1) Dynamic *Qigong* – *Qigong* process in which one obtains the *Chi* (Energy) of the universe with the body in motion. Examples: Tai Chi Chuan, *Bāguàzhǎng* (eight trigram palm), nine ways to capture energy for the body, twelve ways to capture energy for the body, eight exercises for the tendons, etc.

(2) Static *Qigong* – *Qigong* process in which one obtains the *Chi* (Energy) of the universe without moving the body (standing or sitting). Examples: Secret of the six sounds of *Tui Na*, Small Universe Circulation, Great Universe Circulation, *Bào Shù Chūn* (embrace the tree), etc.

Gaikikō

The forms of *Gaikikō* or external *Qigong* therapy are: 水晶氣功 *Qigong* through the crystal; 鍼氣功 *Qigong* through acupuncture; *Shiatsu* with

Qigong – Shioda style; カイロ氣功chiropractic with *Qigong*;術後補助外氣功法 post-surgery external Qigong.

三鍼法　Accupuncture technique with three needles: *Qigong* process in which healing is obtained through the balance of Yin-Yang, conducting the *Chi* of the Universe through three needles. The masters Yoshitsugu Hayashi and 買馬志 (*Măi Mă Zhi)* from China are the highest authorities in this art, which has great results on the treatment of Cerebral Vascular Accidents.

Qigong and crystal (水晶氣功) – The *Chi* of the Universe is introduced into the patient through a crystal stone.

Qigong and acupuncture 鍼氣功 – Application of needles at vital points to restore balance and health. Master Liu Chih Ming, my brother in Tao, is the ultimate authority in this art.

按摩氣功・指圧氣功. Qigong and the Shioda Method of Massage and Shiatsu.　It is not only about *anma*, taoist name, or *shiatsu*, japanese term to refer to the massage. The introduction of *Chi* is performed at the same time as the massage.

Qigong and chiropractic massage カイロ氣功 is used in the treatment of the spine and joints; it is most effective when combined with the application of the *Chi* of the Universe. It is a technique that combines chiropractic, born in the U.S., *seitai* technique, born in Japan, and *Qigong*.

Post-surgical external *Qigong*術後補助外氣功法. After surgery the patient undergoes great damage to their prenatal energy. This *Qigong* technique is recommended in order to speed up the recovery process and heal patients faster.

Since I have mastered this External Therapy *Qigong* Technique 外氣功・功法, I mentor those who are interested in post-surgical recovery.

THE BOOK OF THE PATH AND THE VIRTUE
PHILOSOPHY, PHYSICAL AND MENTAL HEALTH

Many laypeople and researchers untruly say that "The Book of the Path and the Virtue", by Old Master Lao Tzu, is difficult to understand. If everyone understands the teachings of Tao, the technique of introducing the "*Chi*" (*Naikikō* – Internal *Qigong*), as well as the meaning of the *kanji* (ideograms) created by Taoists over 10,000 years ago, everything will become clear and easy to understand.

Thus, this book gives significant value to these three points. It was originally written in Japanese and then translated into a reachable and accessible manner.

The first poem of "The Book of the Path and the Virtue" is very important; is the key to understand great part of its content. So, more pages were devoted to explain it.

Poem One

道可道、非常道

Tao is Tao, it is not eternal

If one thinks about Tao, it will not be
Tao anymore. If you sit still while you
are practicing static *Qigong* (*Naikikō*)
and distract yourself with daydreams,
this is no longer Tao, because both body
and soul must be transformed in order
to achieve it. Let oneself be totally in a
state of *Mu* (void, nothing, inexistence,
Yin), which is achieved with the practice
of static *Qigong* and, when joining Sky,
Man and Earth one shall become true Tao.

If one can understand and practice
internal *Qigong*, one will achieve a state
of serenity and the state of Mu. There will
be no room for evil energy such as the
"disease." Longevity will be obtained and virtue will be incorporated. Get
closer to those who have achieved enlightenment. Without the practice of
static and dynamic *Qigong*, you will not be able to be a "Taoist", a Sacred
Master or enlightened.

名可名、非常名
The name is not eternal

Story told among the Taoists.

"Peachtree"

Observe the peach seed. It cannot be broken in the palm of one's hand. But
if one buries it in the soil, the seed will break itself in pieces and from it a
bud will come out. Observe: from "seed" to "bud". The earth has the Yin
energy. It shows the great power of the Yin energy.

From "seed" to "bud" – it is the same essence but not the same name. Along with the growing process, new leaves come out. From "bud" to "leaves" – the name is not kept either. The plant grows strong, resisting the wind, the rain, scorching sun and storm. It becomes "tree", the flowers bloom and the fruits appear. "Seed, bud, leaf, tree, flower, fruit" - when one thinks it is about a name, it is no longer the same one. A constant change occurs.

It is possible to say the same about people given the proportions. They are born from the union of father (Yang) and mother (Yin), led by Tao.

This baby becomes a child, then a boy, a young man and an elder. The child will not be a "child" forever. Living means going through several hardships: the good or bad experiences help men in their growing process, strengthening the character and making the man worthy, such as the Peachtree.

Although there are always 24 hours in a day, the description of this measure is variable. Now it can be 12 o'clock but an hour later it will be one o'clock. It is the same with the four seasons of the year: It may be spring now, but soon it will be summer.

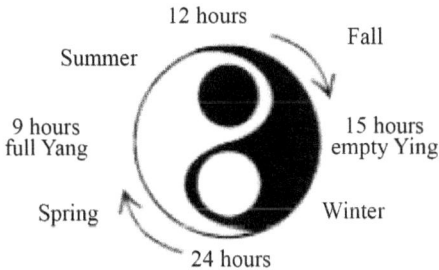

The white part on the left of the Tai Chi figure represents Yang Energy - the existence. The dark part on the right represents Yin Energy - the void. The small circles inside the Tai Chi ball mean there is a third of Yin within Yang and there is also a third of Yang within Yin.

In summary, Yang undergoes transformation when generated, creating Yin, meanwhile Yin undergoes transformation when generated, creating Yang. The full state undergoes transformation when generated, creating the void.

Spring undergoes transformation when generated, creating the summer. "Spring → summer → autumn → winter" - this cycle is in constant mutation, so the name never stays the same.

Grow as worthily as the Peachtree. That is the wish of Taoists for all human beings.

無名天地之始

Cosmos – the beginning of Sky and Earth

The "void" means inexistence and refers to the Cosmos. If we stretch any circle, we will obtain a straight line. The number 1, which is written 一 in *kanji*, comes from the act of "stretching" this circle (Cosmos). It means that it (Yang / Sky) came into existence where there was nothing before. Following this line of thinking, number 2 came as 二, (Yin / Earth). Taoists interpret such numbers this way. The "void" is the origin of "Sky / Yang" and "Earth / Yin" and where everything has begun.

有名万物之母

Mother of all existence (母)

Everything which has a name and exists in the Cosmos is the mother's creation (genitor), therefore the ideogram 母 / haha / has originated from "𝟥" This ideogram created by the ancient Taoists represents the Cosmos or the Great Universe / Tai Chi, as seen below:

The first three circles are linked to /haha/

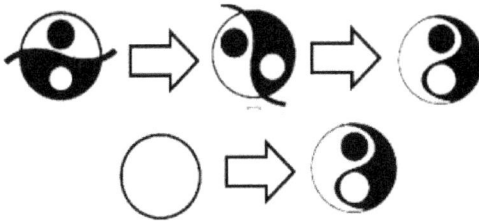

The last two circles are linked to the Void

From the void aforementioned, Sky/Earth and Yang/Yin rise creating everything. For example, in a glass full of water there is no room for anything else. However, if it is empty, there will be room to fill it. Similarly, the Cosmos is made out of empty spaces, where the stars, the Sun (Yang) and the Moon (Yin) were born, - giving birth to the Earth with Yin and Yang in balance. The balance of Yin and Yang in the planet enabled the emergence of our environment and all living things that inhabit it. Everything that has a name is the Mother's (Great Universe) creation. Everything that exists has its reason to be. Everything is equal in the eyes of the Mother". However, because of the selfishness and ambition of some human beings, "Mother Nature" is being destroyed. Taoism, God and the Mother warn: "You cannot destroy nature. Harmonize with nature!"

故常無欲以觀其妙

The continuous detachment reveals the Mystery

Therefore, the "mystery" is appreciated with constant awareness of both the void and the detachment.

"Mystery" (妙) means the occurrence of something mystical, extraordinary.

"Seeing" (観) is not about "seeing with the eyes", but with the mind and the heart, keeping your eyes shut in a state of "void" during static *Qigong* exercise.

By practicing static *Qigong* with determination, giving up the desires and absorbing only the "Postnatal Energy ", one is led to a state of "void" when, mysteriously, the mind begins to see colors and lights. In the union of Sky / Man / Earth by static *Qigong*, the embrace of the "Mother" (Tai Chi) clarifies the "mystery."

常有欲以観其徴

By believing constantly in the existence of *Chi*,

one can see the vital energy point.

In believing that "there is" *Chi* and wishing for the Postnatal Energy, along with the practice of *Qigong*, the "vital energy point" (徴) will be attained. It means, first of all, the existence of something wonderful. It also stands for the "vital point" / *tsubo* / in the Taoist medicine.

The Tai Chi ball, with approximately 8 cm in diameter, is located 3 cm behind the navel and 7 cm in front of the spine. That is the position of the "vital energy point". Even with surgery, this ball cannot be seen. During pregnancy, the fetus develops while receiving *Chi* from that point.

The practice of static *Qigong* causes the union of Yin-Yang in the "vital energy point". Thus, the temperature increase is noticeable - a kind of "warmth" - followed by the sight of something, sometimes a light or glare. At a later stage, it is possible to see the "dragon" (Yang) or "Tiger" (Yin). It is another secret of the Taoist art.

The "Vital energy point" (徴) - is the human center of *Chi*, where the "Prenatal energy" received from the parents is. Life is maintained because *Chi* circulates throughout the body from that point. In order to have a balanced and healthy life, one must preserve the most out of Prenatal

Energy and capture Postnatal Energy daily through the practice of *Qigong*, keeping it always active. "Seeing" the mystery is "seeing" the union of Yin-Yang, *Chi* and the vital energy point.

此兩者同出而異名

Both have the same origin, although they receive different names

"Both" refers to the "mystery" and to the "point of vital energy": Cosmos, Tai Chi, Mother, although they have different names, they are at the origin of the Yin and Yang energies.

同謂之玄

Equally, it is said 玄 (Xuán, obscure)

Both "Mystery" (妙) and "Vital energy point" (徼) represent the Yin-Yang Energies "equally". It is said 玄 (*Xuán*, obscure).

"玄" – *Xuán*

It is what activates the Prenatal Energy, introducing Yang Energy from Sky and Yin Energy from Earth into the Tai Chi ball behind the navel. It is not an exaggeration to say that one cannot understand "The Book of the Path and the Virtue" if one does not understand the meaning of "玄". It is very important, and is a secret of Taoist art that has not yet been disclosed.

Evolution of the *kanji* "玄".

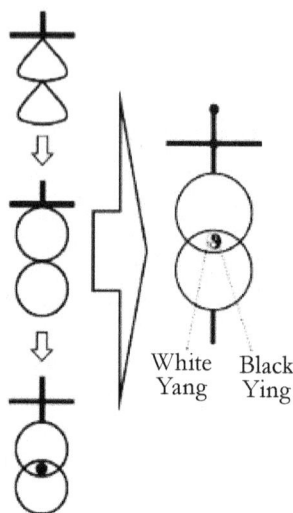

White Yang   Black Ying

The strokes "╋" on the top represent an antenna. The sign ● in the figure ╋ corresponds to the top of the head. In Taoist medicine, that is the point called "*Bǎi Huì*". The sign ● in the center of the figure ✢ corresponds to the hypophysis, which is the size of a rice grain and is located at the base of the brain, between the eyes. Among the Taoists of *Senshu* lineage it is called "Rǔ Bǔ". The two circles under the strokes ╋ represent the upper and lower halves of the body. The stroke "╎" under the circle indicates the point named "*Huì Yín*" by Taoist medicine and "*Yīn Qiāo*" by the *Senshu* lineage. It is considered a very important point.

The strokes "╋" symbolize the capture of Yang and the stroke "-" symbolizes the capture of Yin Energy. The Yin-Yang energies unite at the Tai Chi ball located behind the navel.

"╋" represents the number ten (十) of *kanji*.

Ten refers to: 5 Yin = spleen, liver, heart, lung and kidneys; and 5 Yang = stomach, gall bladder, small intestine, large intestine and bladder.

The maintenance of health and longevity is possible when one reaches the state of void with the practice of static Qigong, capturing the "5 Yin/5 Yang" (5 + 5 = 10).

For capturing the Yang Energy "十" there is 五 雲 透 体 (Five-colored cloud Technique)

Regarding the capture of Yin Energy "｜", there are many Qigong techniques in the "12 ways for capturing energy for the body." Details can be found in the book "Qigong Pai Lin and Chiropractic/Seitai with Energization" (Master Kenichi Shioda).

玄之又玄
Obscure again

With the practice of static and dynamic Qigong, it is possible to reach a state of full void in order to better absorb the Yin and Yang energies from the Universe, meaning Postnatal Energy. This practice should be a daily habit, like all the other human ones, because this Energy is depleted in 24 hours. Man day by day consumes fish, vegetables, meat and fruit that come from the earth. Being the earth Yin Energy, food is as well. If one does not eat those every day, one will be hungry and weak.

In order for such balance to exist, it is also necessary to consume Yang Energy. The body will not feel hungry, but this need can be noticed because of one's tiredness, which will end with the capturing of *Chi* (energy). The daily practice of energizing provides one with a healthy long life

Mountain Wizards and Sacred Masters get up early and practice the exercises of *Senshu* Taoism until around 11 am.

I practice it for about 5-6 hours a day and I can say that the feeling when a moment of complete peace is achieved, with the introduction of *Chi*, is indescribable: "I feel an unmatched happiness and maternal love."

衆妙之門
Portal of Mystery

Through the comprehension and practice of 玄 (*Xuán*, obscure), humans will feel the mystery. This is the path to something that can be named "The Portal of Wonders".

玄 is the source of an infinite quantity of Yin-Yang and it is also full of Pre and Postnatal Energy. If one practices static and dynamic Qigong one will be closer to the "Portal".

The "Portal" is the entrance to achieving good health, longevity, spiritual elevation, peace, happiness and love. Equally, it is the "gateway" to becoming a mountain wizard or a sacred Taoist.

妙 "Mystery"

Due to being a subject of great importance, the following explanation must be well understood. The ideogram 妙 is composed by 女 (woman) plus 少 (little young). Therefore, it might be interpreted, with agglutination of the senses, as "young woman". By practicing static Qigong, Young Energy, the new Postnatal Energy, is captured when the state of void is achieved. This is the way to experience the "Mystery" and "Embrace" of the "Mother" (Great Universe).

Poem Two

Beauty thinks and knows that it is beautiful. This is a misconception, a mistake. For example, imagine the existence of two varieties of flower, each claiming to be the most beautiful among all. Since this concept is relative and variable, given those who analyze, every human being who assesses these flowers has their own opinion, when, in fact, both are beautiful, as are all creations of Tao, the Universe and motherhood.

Kindness is also recognized as such by everyone. If a wise man talks about it everyone will be convinced. Still, if another wise man discusses about another kind of kindness, people will believe, likewise. If there is a difference in the content said by both wise men, people will not know which one is the true kindness and therefore they will be confused about evil. So, when can one say what is good or evil? "It is kindness! It is kindness "- if one cries that out all the time, the opposite, evil, will be born. It is part of the law of nature to bring up the evil when kindness reaches its maximum degree.

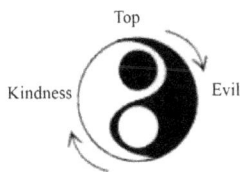

Master Lao Tzu once said to Master Confucius: "You should not talk all the time about "good" or "wisdom". People get increasingly apprehensive, insecure and hesitant. Eventually it will turn into evil." Thereafter, Master Confucius corrected himself. It is a well-known episode among the Taoists.

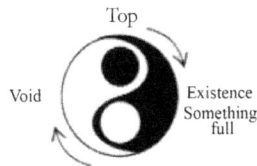

Therefore, the "existence" or the "void" originate in a reciprocal act. "Existence" and "Void" are always born and transformed in an eternal, circular and uninterrupted motion.

However, the "existence" is not eternal. One day it will become extinct. It will disappear. But at some point it will rise again from the "void".

The same happens with "difficulty" and "ease". Both complement each other and even when difficulty reaches its highest degree, so does the ease. Difficult and easy things complement each other.

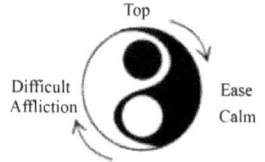

Let us take for example the antonym words "affliction" and "calm". During one's life there are countless "afflictions" yet, by enduring and overcoming them comes peace. One cannot give up halfway. That is what we all know.

"Long" and "short" compare to each other and "high" and "low" complete each other. Both "long" and "short" have positive and negative sides. For example, something can be good because it is long, but it can also be bad because it is exceeding. In the same way, something can be good because it is short, or it can be bad because it lacks something. In everything, there are two sides and we must learn to recognize them.

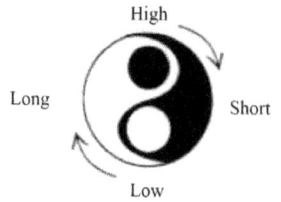

"High" (sky) and "Low" (ground) also complete each other. How would one exist without the other? For example, it is correct to say that "the mountain is high" simply because it was erected by the supporting base (low). If there were no foothills, the mountain itself would not exist.

Do not be presumptuous feeling noble. Only by the existence of a humble class it is possible for one to call oneself notable. Tao preaches equality among peoples and mutual help.

"Sound" and "Voice" constitute harmony. That is to say: "Sound": Rain, wind, waves, sounds of the river; "Voice": insects, birds, animals.

Both "sound" and "voice" are products of the Mother. They are products of "Tao / the Mother", constituting the natural harmony. The "sounds" or "voices" of nature soothe people's hearts.

There is only the "front" because there is the "rear". Both also complete each other. Therefore, the "Holy Master" lets nature take its course. To let nature act by itself - it is the best teaching of Tao.

One practices the teaching of the "speechless". "Tao / the Mother" created everything yet never pronounced itself in "words", it is born and does not appropriate things. Even if it is helpful it does not expect any reward. Even if it accomplishes something, it does not remain. It only unifies Sky, man and Earth, but it will not remain. Thus, the thought about the theory of "Tao, Yin-Yang" shall never change.

"美" – Beauty

About the two upper dots " ＼ ／": the dot on the left side represents Yin Energy and the right dot represents Yang Energy. The strokes "王" which are written in the center symbolize sky, man, earth united by "|". The strokes "大" on the lower part of the *kanji* symbolize: "ノ" – The Yang Energy descending from sky to earth. "＼" indicates the Yin Energy, existing on Earth, rising to sky. This way, the *kanji* for human being, that is, "人", was created by ancient Taoists.

Nature is made in a cycle: rain falls from sky, reaching the earth. The sun, shining upon the surface, turns water into steam, which returns to sky. By adding the horizontal stroke "一" to the *kanji* "人", one obtains "大" (great, huge). This horizontal stroke "一" represents the Cosmos, the Universe.

The Yin-Yang Energies of the Universe, captured when man becomes "one" with Sky and Earth, transform him into a "beautiful" being, physically well-formed and healthy.

"To be sacred" means to have the elevated spiritual level of those who have reached Tao. Beautiful on the inside and on the outside.

Poem three

A truly wise man has no appreciation for the goods which are considered precious or valuable. His fights never cease, not because he tries to overcome others or become wiser than everyone else, but because such things are not dear to him.

不尚賢、使民不爭。不貴難得之貨、使民不為盜。不見可欲、使民心不乱。是以聖人之治、虛其心、実其腹、弱其志、強其骨。常使民無知無欲、使夫知者不敢為也。為無為、則無不治。

The people shall not steal money and goods, which are considered hard to obtain, as they are not valued. People end up losing themselves or becoming slaves of greed because they accumulate money and treasures. Misery is planted, the mind is disturbed and one ends up doing evil deeds. Because of all that, the great master teaches us that the way for the people to live in peace is "to empty the mind".

In order to empty the mind, one recommends the practice of static Qigong: one begins by leaving the mind empty in order to receive the *Chi* and make the stomach full. "Full stomach" means, as it was explained in "玄", to introduce Yin and Yang energies into the "徼" (vital Energy point)/ "ᵇ". By weakening the appetite for greed and strengthening the bones (body) with static Qigong, there will be good physical and mental health.

The "powerful ones" who rule the world should guide the people on the path of humility and detachment. In order to do so, it is necessary for the ruler to give an example, so everyone can live in harmony with nature, knowing Tao, without being "clever" or greedy. The world will know peace if it maintains the "natural state" and detachment.

"ノ" represents " 𝟛 ", while "田" represents the "net". The Cosmos is full of Energy in infinite amounts, like a thin net. Another of the Taoist teachings is the ideogram "薪" (firewood). It means the state of piled up firewood. "ノ ﹗ ﹗ ヽ" indicates "fire", "heat", that is, "Yang Energy". The practice of static Qigong requires an "empty" mind and the capture of " ノ ﹗ ﹗ ヽ", fire/Yang Energy. It will make the " 𝟛 ", the Tai Chi ball, warm up.

By warming up it will make the Energy circulate like a net through the body, which constitutes a small Cosmos. The practice provides longevity and does not allow for diseases (evil) to establish.

People contract the "false fever" when they are annoyed or upset. The increase of the false fever causes the "burning" of all the "firewood" 田, which leads to diseases and even death.

"Being empty" 無 is the secret and source of the search of the Taoists. When one achieves the state of "void" 無 with the practice of static Qigong, one starts to feel an indescribable well-being. One feels that "life is wonderful" with the feeling of "love and peace". Taoists wish for everyone to reach this stage. The study of Tao and its practices is also recommended.

Unlike many, who only believe in what they can see with their own eyes, Taoists believe in the "void" 無, which cannot be seen. Reaching this state when practicing static Qigong means seeing something like, for example, the "glare", the "light". One starts to be aware of everything, which leads to the elevation of the character. Only with the practice of static Qigong one can reach the state of void "無", in which pre and postnatal Energies can be found, for that is the world of Truth.

The true luminosity can only be seen when one is completely in a state of "無". The "徼" (point of vital Energy) "Tai Chi ball, " 𝟛 ", starts to pulsate like that of a baby; in this stage, a feeling that "life is wonderful" arises, but not everyone is able to feel or understand such pleasure.

The kanji "無" has 12 strokes, equivalent to 12 meridians, 6 Yin and 6 Yang.

O >> Indicates the Void for Taoists. According to that thought, within the Void there is Yin, with its 5 Energies (directed towards the lungs, kidneys, liver, heart and spleen) and Yang with other 5 Energies (large intestine, bladder, gall bladder, small intestine and stomach).

O >> Therefore, 5+5 = "10 Energies" are absorbed from the Cosmos in the practice of static Qigong. Taoists affirm that this is a true treasure. The true treasure and true happiness are born if the great universe and the small universe are united.

In Taoism one also says that within "nothing or void" lies everything, like in a storage area. It is a "paradox" in which everything can be created, with the existence of Yin-Yang Energies. If it is full, nothing can fit inside and nothing can be created.

空
·
虛

>> Everything is created because in the Great Universe there are the "Yin-Yang Energies". From them come the stars, the Sun (Yang Energy), the Moon (Yin Energy) and, finally, living beings.

For a life in harmony with nature, one must not want more than one needs. Between "money/treasure" and "health/longevity", which one is more important?

"Life is swift, and the money spent in a lifetime is also swift. Therefore, do not wish to have more than necessary." These are words by Master *Liu Pai Lin*.

If we become "humble" and "detached", humankind will conquer "peace" and "happiness", building a better world.

Poem four

Tao is like a recipient of infinite size, empty and indistinct. The "Void" is shaped like a circle, like the Cosmos, and even when we put everything in it (stars, among other things) it will not be full. It is endlessly deep, like an abyss.

It can be described as the main stem of everything; it sobers up the sagacity of all things, turns to dust, dims the light, and neutralizes the waste with the harmony of "Yin and Yang Energies".

When it comes to the human body, which is a small Universe, Tao weakens the disease, dissolving the tumor, which resembles lumped dust.

帝之先。　塵。湛兮似或存。吾不知誰之子。象　宗。挫其銳、解其粉、和其光、同其　道沖而用之或不盈。淵兮似万物之

It radiates light with Yang Energy, trying to harmonize the Yin-Yang. Illnesses are expelled or neutralized.

When the Yin and Yang Energies are balanced, everything happens without

troubles throughout life. Take celestial bodies as an example, because they carry on without problems, observing the laws of nature, being part of it. One can say the same about the human body.

One can live safely, happily and healthily, maintaining longevity, if there is harmony of Yin-Yang.

There is no way to determine the origin of Tao. However, it is more primordial than the emperor who rules the people.

"帝" – Sovereign, emperor

"亠" is like the lid of a pan. It corresponds, in the Cosmos, to its upper part or, like Taoists say, the "lid".

Right below "丶 丿": the left stroke represents Yin and the right stroke represents Yang. The strokes "冖" mean the unification of everything.

"巾" Yang Energy (Sky) and Yin Energy (Earth) are offered to all the peoples, both in north-south and in east-west, and "丨" indicates the direction in the sky-earth orientation. They bring endless happiness and peace.

Finally, the ancient Taoists created the *kanji* "帝" with the meaning of person who knows Tao and the "virtue" and, living close to nature without artifices, rules the people thinking about everyone's happiness and peace.

Poem five

Sky and earth do not possess what the people know as "仁" (benevolent respect), that is, the feeling of wishing well, deep compassion, love. Therefore, even though it creates everything, men are like straw dogs, which will later be left aside. Sacred masters are also impassive. They let all men act freely. They do not think about elevating passivity, or argue about the concept of "仁", questioning the answers. Also the peasants, treated like the dog made of straw, cultivate food and consume it.

Everything which exists "disappears" and out of "nothing" comes something. The relationship between Sky and Earth resembles the bellows, tool used by the blacksmith to rekindle the fire. The bellows is hollow on the inside. There is nothing. Like it was already explained in the first poem, out of nothing one can create everything, that is, "Mother of everything that can be named". Due to being hollow, something has an unbreakable spirit. With Yin and Yang Energics it is possible to be natural and free. The more one moves the bellows, the more it expels wind. The strength of the wind existing in Sky and Earth is ruled by the Energy of endless starts. All living beings receive these winds, which Taoists believe come from the stars.

One must never bend to excessively sweet and empty words. Excessive and empty talking causes exhaustion. Let things happen naturally. Practice static Qigong and protect the prenatal Energy existing in the Tai Chi ball. With that, one can live a free life, being able to feel the love cradled by mother-nature.

"仁" – Respect, love, charity

"イ" – Indicates the human being; "二" – the upper stroke indicates Sky 天 and the lower stroke indicates earth 地. The human being, becoming one with sky and earth, begins to cultivate the feelings contained in the *kanji* "仁".

Stars		Wind
Sun	Indicate	Fire – Yang Energy
Moon		Water – Yin Energy

Straw dog

Made of straw and shaped like a dog, it is an ornament used in rituals during festivals, put over the altar in order to exorcize evil.

Bellows

Device shaped like a box, used by blacksmiths in order to rekindle the fire and melt metals in the m ' ' ' ' and swords.

Poem six

Like God, the spirit of the valley never perishes. Its name is *genbin*, and its gate is the root of sky and earth. It continues its infinite existence, always young, and with this youth it is never extinguished.

"谷" – Valley

The left side of "ノ丶" indicates the Yang Energy and the right side indicates the Yin Energy; "人": the Yin-Yang Energies descend from the Cosmos into lakes and valleys; "口": a certain place, which indicates the valley itself "谷". The Yin-Yang Energies descend from the Cosmos into the valley and shall be eternal, like God.

"神"– God

谷神不死。是謂玄牝。玄牝之門、是謂天地之根。緜緜若存、用之不勤。

Omnipresent figure, which has created the Universe.

ネ indicates 示 (God, deity);

申 indicates the field, the rice field.

48

Indicates center,
axis

申>> the central stroke in this *kanji* has the upper part thicker and the lower part thinner. The upper part absorbs the Yang Energy of Sky and the lower part absorbs the Yin Energy of earth. At the same time, the thinner lower part represents the action of the Energy of sky, earth, fire (Sun) and water, resulting in the development of the rice fields, vegetables and fruits, while herbs, flowers and trees grow. Man, birds, animals and fish shall live eternally, being born and transforming. It is the reason why one says: God is nature, God is the universe, sky, earth. Due to the existence of God, the universe and all things also exist.

"玄牝" – Genbin; Xuán Pìn

The *kanji* "玄" (*Xuán*, obscure) was explained in the first poem. However, we have given more details about secrets of Taoism below.

Yin-Yang "牝" (bin/mesu)

"牝" (*mesu* = female). The great master has compared woman 女 to the female this way: "Woman" 女= Yin. "〈" indicates Yin Energy. "ノ" indicates Yang Energy/precipitation.

The stroke "一" unites the Yin-Yang Energies. Thus was formed the *kanji* for woman (女) .

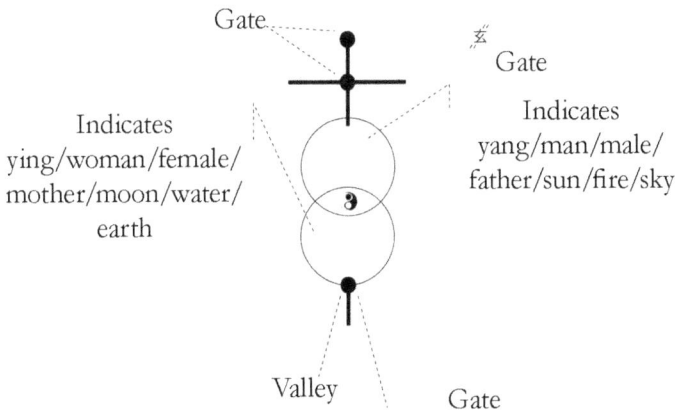

Just like there is the Yang Energy door, Yin Energy also has a door. It is called "*Huì Yin*" in oriental medicine, and in Taoist medicine, it is called "*Yīn Qiāo*". The great master has compared this point to the "valley". Since the valley is on earth, it is "Yin", and by capturing the Energy of the sun, it can continue to exist indefinitely. From the lake water springs, it runs through the valleys, allowing the development of herbs, flowers, trees, birds. Consequently the mountain wizards also choose the surroundings of the valley for their dwelling place.

The stroke on the left side of the *kanji* woman (女), that is, "ノ", becomes thinner from the top down. It represents menstruation, the impurity of the blood being expelled. It also represents the food which grows under the earth (Yin), like the turnip, the carrot, the burdock. All of them have a shape (upper part thicker and lower part thinner) which indicates the development towards the underground.

Poem seven

Sky shall exist throughout eternity. The earth shall continue to exist forevermore. Both are eternal because they have let themselves be at the mercy of natural laws without striving to survive. Therefore, they can live very long in time and space. Following their example, the sacred masters, too, with no fuss, withdraw. They do not try to draw attention, but live in silence, absorbed in thought. They practice static Qigong and reach the state of "void", abandoning every worldly thought. Consequently, they achieve virtue and reach the objective of Tao, with health and longevity.

其無私邪。故能成其私。
以其不自生。故能長生。是以聖人、
天長地久。天地所以能長且久者、
後其身而身先、外其身而身存。非以

"生" – To be born, to create

The Energy of the Cosmos provides a long life (生).

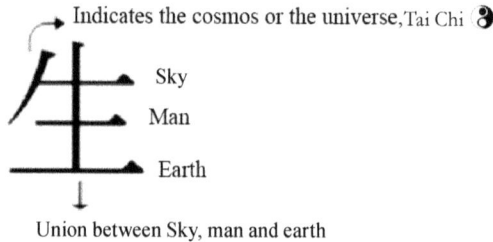

Indicates the cosmos or the universe, Tai Chi ☯

生
Sky
Man
Earth

Union between Sky, man and earth

天長地久
Long sky, eternal earth

"Sky" (天) – indicates the long (Yang). It refers to man, emperor. "Earth" (地) – indicates eternity (Yin). It refers to woman, empress. In Japan, there were times when one said "*Tenchôsetsu*" (天長節 – knot of longevity of sky/emperor), referring to the emperor's birthday, and "*Chikyusetsu*" (地久節) – knot of eternity of earth/empress), the empress' birthday.

Poem eight

The best asset is like water: it benefits everything and everyone and does not do them any harm; it descends to the remotest place, where most do not like to be, and there it remains. Therefore, it can be affirmed that it is an existence which resembles Tao. A good place for water to remain is where it can find absolute calm, like the bottom of an abyss.

May everyone benefit from affection and love, for those words are true where righteousness and peace reign.

The phenomena carry the strength of transformation. When necessary, receive celestial grace. Foreseeing a good opportunity to act, rain falls offering fresh and divine waters.

善能、動善時。　夫唯不争、故無尤。
善淵、与善仁、言善信、正善治、事
衆人之所悪。　故幾於道。居善地、心
上善若水。　水善利万物而不争、処

Water only brings benefits to all, never harming or competing – therefore it never receives criticism.

"水" – Water

On the stroke "亅" in the center of the *kanji*, the top indicates Yang / Sun while the bottom indicates Yin / earth. The end of the stroke faces up to indicate that the water falls from sky towards Earth, and with the heat of the Sun upon the Earth, it turns into steam and rises again to sky.

"フ" - the Yang Energy, the sun and the fire come down from Sky to the Earth. Therefore, the stroke narrows at the tip; " く " – the Yin Energy and the water flow to places increasingly lower. The final part of the stroke is thicker " 丶 " because they descend and settle down in low places.

Taoist teaching

To be humble like water, which always looks for the lowest places; to always keep a sense of respect for others, becoming someone who behaves in a simple manner, as someone who has no possessions, in a natural attitude. To live loosely as a useless tree, which, when having lived a thousand years becomes worshiped as a "tree of God."

The tree whose wood has much use, will certainly be cut in no time. Take as an example the useless tree; practice static Qigong and have a long life. Thus, one will gain "respect" as a "deity" or "holiness."

其無私邪
Attachment (free of attachment)

Practice static Qigong freeing oneself, keeping the mind empty and abandoning any impious thoughts.

A person who appears to be humble but has undue pride, being arrogant, greedy and with no character is nothing but a fool.

Poem nine

One should not fill the recipient, for it shall overflow.
The sword and other cutting tools, when too sharp, shall not last a long time because they will end up breaking. If one collects a lot of money or property, one shall be subject to the greed of thieves and shall not be able to keep it. Becoming rich and eminent and filling oneself up with vanity shall attract misfortune. If one has some success, one should retire and live joining Sky and Earth - that is the way.

"金" - currency, money or precious metals which shine in shades of gold

The upper part of the *kanji*, " 人" indicates the Cosmos; "干" the upper stroke indicates

Sky (Yang) and the lower indicates Earth (Yin), being the vertical line "|" the junction and an indicative that it descends to the underground. " 丷 " or " ≗ " mean that treasures lie underground.

"The path of the Cosmos"

The path of the Cosmos is one that is climbed step by step, starting from nothing and advancing through effort. And one retreats observing the time to retire.
Human greed is startling. They always want more and more, not realizing the possibility of withering, not only physically, but also emotionally.

The true "Gold / Prenatal Energy (*Zhen Chi*) is in the Tai Chi ball located 3 cm behind the navel. The Postnatal Energy is gathered at the Tai Chi ball- a real treasure for Taoism, obtained from the Cosmos with the practice of static Qigong.
Do not struggle too much. If one achieves fortune or reasonable recognition, practice static Qigong, capture the Postnatal Energy and have a long and healthy life. Even though one leaves fortune to one's descendants, it certainly shall not bring them happiness.

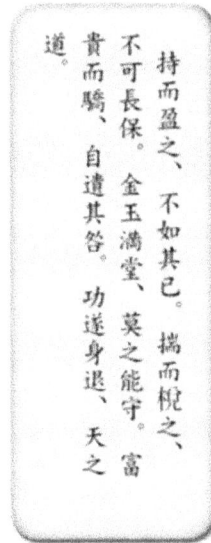

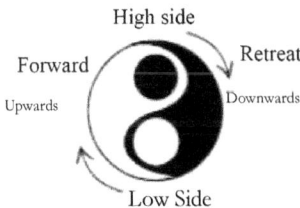

Poem ten

Do not disperse the Energy assimilated by *Yin Qiāo* (Yin Energy input point). Join sky and earth, focusing on capturing the Energy in a relaxed and flexible way, like a baby on its mother's lap. Be relaxed before the Cosmos, *Xuán* (玄), source of Yin and Yang Energies, eliminating the impious thoughts.

In order to avoid errors during the practice, be completely relaxed and exercise static Qigong without thinking: as if you were governing a nation with love for its people; stay at ease, protecting and loving yourself, purifying the troubled soul and controlling health.

載營魄抱一、能無離乎。專気致柔、能嬰児乎。滌除玄覽、能無疵乎。愛民治国、能無為乎。天門開闔、能為雌乎。明白四達、能無知乎。生之、畜之。生而不有、為而不恃、長而不宰。是謂玄德。

The point at the top of the head is called *Bǎi Hui* and the one between the eyebrows is called *Tian Men* (Gate of the Cosmos).

Once this gate is opened, Yang Energy (man, male) penetrates and reaches *Ling Tai* (third ventricle). The input point of Yin Energy is called *Dì Mèn* and by "opening" this point, it is possible to introduce the Yin Energy (woman, female). *Tian Men* and *Dì Mén* are united, so are man and woman, male and female, Yin and Yang. The Energy of the Cosmos must achieve the four chambers named: *Ling Tai* (Yang), *Yin Qiao* (Yin), *Yuán Shen* (Yang central point) and *Ming Men* (Yin central point).

Leading Yin - Yang energies into the four chambers is one of the Secrets of Taoism. Assimilate the technique of Qigong, which allows the achieving of the state of *Mu* (void). Make Energy sprout from the four chambers, cultivating and protecting them; do not think about your "Existence", do not count on it nor control it. Become one with sky and earth, cradled by the mother, and introduce the Energy in a state of total void.

Someone united to the Yin-Yang, sky and earth, is called *"Xuán Dé"*, someone who shows refinement and nobility of character. Practice static Qigong and improve the union of Sky (Yang), man and Earth (Yin) and be a *"Xuán Dé "*.

"明" - Clear, evident; power of reading everything that goes on and happens; glare

The *kanji* "日" means sun. It indicates Yang Energy »»

The *kanji* "月" means moon. It indicates Yin Energy »»

The sun (Yang) and the moon (Yin) are united to illumir   thing.

"抱" 一 - Embracing the number One

Cosmos is considered a ball (○), and is also represented as "zero." If we stretch what is round we will have the 1; therefore, embracing the "1" means "embracing the Cosmos." The Taoist Qigong technique called *"Pau Shu Zhuan"* (embracing the tree in upright posture), is one of the ways "to embrace the Cosmos". This technique is found in the book "Qigong Pai Lin and Chiropractic / Seitai with Energization ", released in 2007.

The four chambers' positions

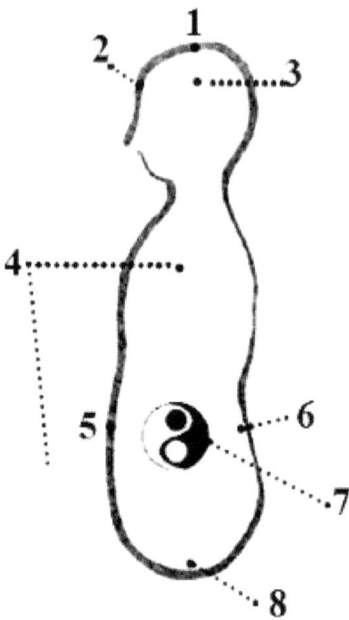

1 – Bǎi Huì

2 – Yìn Táng

3 – Líng Tái

4 – Yuán Shén
(point between the nipples)

5 – navel

6 – Mìng Mén

7 – Tai Chi (Tāi Yuán Xué)

8 – Yīn Qiāo

Like a baby

The Energy of the Cosmos is introduced into the baby through the fontanelle (soft spot), connecting *Ling Tai* and *Yin Qiao* and making pulse occur at the navel, uniting Yin-Yang in the Tai Chi ball (*Tāi Yuán Xué*) and cultivating nutritious Energy. The baby thinks nothing. It is the live image of "naturalness".

Taoists advice: take babies as an example. But adults are incapable of behaving like babies. Therefore, one needs to practice static Qigong and open the *Tian Men* (celestial gate) and *Dì Men* (terrestrial gate), uniting Yin-Yang, by making the Tai Chi ball pulse (*Tāi Yuán Xué*) and striving to preserve Prenatal Energy (*Zhen Chi*) and absorb the Postnatal Energy.

Poem eleven

In a wheel, 30 spokes converge to the center. Between the wheel and the center there is nothing. The empty space and the existence of the spokes make it useful.

By mixing the clay, pots and containers are produced. Their use is possible thanks to the empty space inside them. In houses, rooms with doors and windows are built; however it is the empty space that allows their use. If they are full of objects, they cannot be used.

三十輻共一轂。当其無、有車之用。
埏埴以為器。当其無、有器之用。
鑿户牖以為室。当其無、有室之用。故
有之以為利、無之以為用。

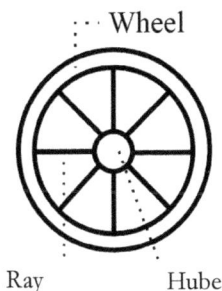

Wheel

Ray   Hube

Therefore, the "void" (*Mu*) makes some objects useful, as it does to the very existence of the human being.

"ノ" represents "🌓", "⊞" represents the cosmic "network" where wood and coal pile up, and " ▸▸▸▸ " indicates the "fire", the "heat", that is, "Yang Energy."

From nothing comes something. From "nothing", "existence" happens. "All things" are created. The body heats up while practicing static Qigong. With fire (▸▸▸▸) that kindles in coal or wood, it is possible to create multiple objects or cook food. There is nothing in the Cosmos, it is an empty space. Being empty is the reason why everything fits. If it is full, nothing shall fit.

Then came the stars, the sun, the moon, the Earth and all beings who live in it, by the dynamics of Yin-Yang.

In Taoism, our body is known as Small Universe. Join together the

Great Universe and the Small Universe, annul oneself in a natural attitude, becoming empty and, in a quiet posture, introduce "*Chi*" (energy). If one does so, something will occur. One begins to feel the "*Chi*", one sees the Mystery (妙) and the "vital Energy point "(微). One feels the Maternal love (Cosmos) and true happiness is achieved.

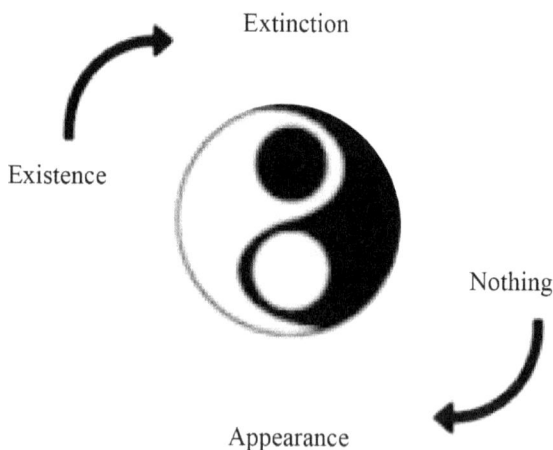

Extinction

Existence

Nothing

Appearance

Poem twelve

'The exuberant colors blind the eyes. The beautiful sound deafens the ears. The abundance and good food spoil taste.

Enjoying the hunt and running through the fields with horses make the heart stony and proud, making feelings lose their way.

Searching blindly for material goods impairs the right actions that are innate in man. Keeping this in mind, the Sacred Master practices static Qigong and supplies Energy into the Tai Chi Ball. There is no interest in beautiful colors, beautiful sounds and hearty meals. So greed is abandoned and the teachings of Tao are followed and observed.

五色令人目盲。五音令人耳聾。五味令人口爽。馳騁畋獵、令人心發狂。難得之貨、令人行妨。是以聖人、為腹不為目。故去彼取此。

"五" number five

It represents the number five and also:

Taoism - Five Element Theory of Yin and Yang

Elements	Colors	Tastes	Organs (Yin)	Bowels (Yang)
Wood	Green	Sour	Liver	Gall bladder
Fire	Red	Bitter	Heart	Small intestine
Earth	Yellow	Sweet	Spleen	Stomach
Metal	White	Spicy	Lungs	Large intestine
Water	Black	Salty	Kidney	Bladder

This figure represents the "evolution" of the *kanji*. Taoism says "All the colors of nature are beautiful. See a flower, for example. The sounds produced by nature are pleasant, like the chirping of birds or the murmuring of rivers. They are wonderful!

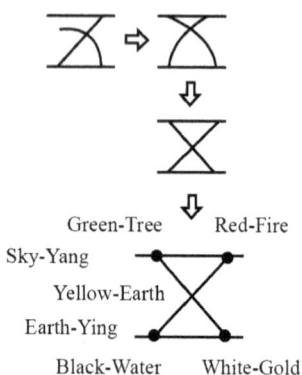

Green-Tree   Red-Fire
Sky-Yang
Yellow-Earth
Earth-Ying
Black-Water   White-Gold

All foods produced by nature are tasty. For example, we have fruit, honey etc. Binge eating, as every excessive act, spoils the taste and causes diseases. Do not get carried away by too much enthusiasm or passion. Always act with moderation.

Practice internal and static Qigong as the Taoists and Sacred masters do; please the stomach with "*Chi*" and ask yourself where the real goods and treasures hide.

Poem thirteen

Men are astonished when they are admired and conquer glory, and even when they are ashamed they are astonished. That is because they think that Glory and Shame are the largest and most interesting events. What startles them in the face of Glory or Shame?

Men see Glory as superior and Shame as inferior. Before Glory they are scared and apprehensive. Before Shame, they are disappointed and apprehensive. Both Glory and Shame are considered astonishments in Taoism. And what do they see as glorifying or shameful? Which parameter is used when one talks about ennobling and worrisome events?

寵辱若驚。貴大患若身。何謂寵辱
若驚。寵為上、辱為下。得之若驚、
失之若驚。是謂寵辱若驚。何謂貴大
患若身。吾所以有大患者、為吾有身。
及吾無身、吾有何患。故貴以身為天
下、乃可寄天下。愛以身為天下、乃
可託天下。

All this happens because the highest interest is concentrated on Glory and Shame. When there is no interest in mind, there will be no room for apprehension, worry or misfortune.

Therefore, do not build a world in which something is considered as glorifying to oneself or do not create such thoughts in mind; do not build a world in which one desires to lean on. Dedicate oneself body and soul to the practice of static Qigong. Whoever loves Nature, the Mother and God shall find true love and happiness by surrendering to them.

"大" – Great

It was already explained in the second poem, in the excerpt of the *kanji* "美" (beauty, beautiful), but here it will be explained in more detail.

The stroke "ノ" indicates the Yang energy, male.

From the sky, the solar rays are directed to the earth, illuminating and feeding all with Yang Energy.

The stroke ヽ indicates Yin Energy, the female.

From the sky, rain falls towards Earth.

The stroke points up meaning that the rain rushes down to earth. The sun, in turn, illuminates and heats the soil with its Yang Energy and makes water go up to the sky again as steam.

The strokes, together, make the *kanji* "人" (person). The Yin Energy (female, wife) and Yang (male, husband) help and support one another, walking in harmony with the Tao.

By adding "一" (one) to "人" there is the union of Yin-Yang, male-female, making the *kanji* "大" (great). One conquers the "Great" happiness due to the fact that the couple lives in harmony, helping each other.

Glory and shame

The news in the world only exhibit glorious and shameful acts or crimes. Not showing interest in these situations and practicing the union of Sky / Man / Earth through static Qigong generates the "Great" happiness.

Poem fourteen

Even if one fixes one's gaze, Tao cannot be seen. It is what we call "formless object" (invisible). Even if one tries to listen, one does not hear. It is what we call "silent object" (inaudible).

Tao is nature, the void, the energy; one cannot touch it even if one wants to. We say that it is something intangible. Even if one wants to clarify these three elements, it is almost impossible.

Tao is the fusion of the three. Above it, there is Yang Energy, but one cannot clarify it. It cannot be evidenced. Below it, there is Yin Energy, but, since it lies in darkness, one cannot notice it.

視之不見、名曰夷。聽之不聞、名
曰希。搏之不得、名曰微。此三者不
可致詰。故混而為一。其上不皦、其
下不昧。繩繩不可名、復歸於無物。
是謂無狀之狀、無物之象。是謂惚恍。
迎之不見其首、隨之不見其後。執古
之道、以御今之有。能知古始、是謂
道紀

For example, one cannot know what lies in the dark / Yin / earth and which things will arise. Will it be insects, plants, flowers, animals or men? They grow and go up. When they reach the peak, they descend. When they descend, one does not know which form they will assume.

Light / Top/ Yang/ Sky

Dark / Lower/ Yin / Earth

All beings perish. The only thing we can affirm is that Yin and Yang are in endless motion; therefore one cannot name them. For example, a man does not keep the same name forever. He changes: baby - child – boy – young boy – lad - man - elder - death. The same name is not kept. That is what is found in Chapter 1 "The name is the name, the name is not eternal."

Clockwise, starting from the bottom (赤子), we have: Baby - Child - Youngster – Lad – Man - Elder - Demise.

Finally, back to nothing that is Yin. Tao is infinite and it is always reborn. That is called formless form, imageless image. It is a natural state without artifice that transcends time.

Tao does not try to see and follow the process of transformation of the beginning of Yin and Yang. This change that persists since ancient times follows its path.

Taoists know well the beginning and essence of Tao.

"視" – To see

礻	見
示 — Sky, Earth, Ying, Central trace, Yang	⊖ — Sky, Earth

The circle indicates Cosmos or Tai Chi. The upper stroke inside the circle indicates the sky, and the lower one indicates the earth. - Eye of the Cosmos, final limit. The Energy of Yin is on earth " ∟ " and with the dynamics of Sky / Yang / sun it returns to the sky " ⌐ ".

In Cosmos as in sky and on earth, there are the Yin and Yang Energies and Yang Energy illuminates the earth / Yin. The earth / Yin, which received radiation from Yang, returns to the sky and is reborn. With this, one can "see" nature and all objects.

In the twentieth and twenty-first centuries, the atom, elementary particle, quarks, are being studied by scientists. However, the *"Chi"* that scientists call the "Energy" is still in the early stages of its elucidation.

Regarding cars powered by solar energy, according to Taoist precepts, its good performance is due to the bodywork, which represents the Yin, while solar energy represents the Yang.

Thus, the union of Yin and Yang occurs. It is one of the research results about *"Chi"* and it can be given a small merit by not causing environmental pollution, although it would be better if cars did not exist.

儿

With the convenience of the car, people stop walking and that causes diseases.

Poem fifteen

Since ancient times, Taoists who master Tao know the secrets of Yin – Yang well. In Taoism there are seven levels of deep teachings and Taoists master them all. The knowledge and wisdom of the Taoists can be compared to the act of crossing a river in winter.

They cross it attentively and carefully, observing the river beforehand. They have a cautious attitude that resembles that of a small country surrounded by powerful countries.

They are like the guest who is welcomed with all solemnity. Calm, they are like ice slowly melting in early spring. Simple as a tree devoid of exuberance. They are like the wide valley without remnants of petty thoughts. They are obscure like the muddy water which becomes clean as it is left undisturbed.

Is there someone like the Taoists who have the stillness and the ability to transform like the water that gradually purifies itself?

Taoists who preserve this Tao do not desire satisfaction from material things. They are satisfied with the bare minimum. Therefore, the Taoists do not cling to greed or try to do something new.

They are steady and follow the teachings that have existed since ancient times, without thinking, saying or acting against them and joining Sky and Earth, cradled in maternal love.

"古" - Old, long time

The upper part indicates the number ten (十). In the Sky conceived by Taoism there are "ten Energies", five of which consisting of "Yin Energies" and the other five consisting of "Yang Energies", also known as *"Shí Qiān"*, which means:

Yang = *kinoe hinoe tsuchinoe kanoe mizunoe*
Yin = *kinoto hinoto tsuchinoto kanoto mizunoto*
Go gyo = *tree fire earth gold water*

"口" (*kuchi* = mouth) indicates the Great Universe and the small universe. Tao is the Great Universe and our body is the small universe.

Since ancient times, Taoists have been capturing the "ten Energies", henceforth introducing the Postnatal Energy into the body (Yin), which is the small universe, leading it through the hypophysis, tongue, throat and chest all the way to the Tai Chi ball (*Tāi Yuán Xué*). By doing so they guarantee the spiritual elevation and the maintenance of a long life.

塾能濁以静之徐清。塾能安以動之徐生

If fresh Postnatal Energy is not introduced daily, the human body is filled with maleficent energy. Master Lao Tzu, in order to make comprehension easier, used the word "dim" (濁) referring to maleficent energy.

One introduces the Cosmos' Postnatal Energy in order to eliminate the "dim" energy trapped in the body, purifying oneself (清) little by little (徐). To do so, one can use the Qigong technique in which one makes the energies flow through the *Xiǎo Zhōu Tiān* (small universe) and the practice of static Qigong. In the state of "void", the movement of real *Chi* (Energy) is born, which purifies maleficent energy (dim), turning it into pure "water" (Energy), making the body healthy.

"満たす" – To fill

It is something that can be said about everything, but if one tries to fill (satisfy) oneself with greed, in the end one will lose. Do not try to satisfy yourself beyond necessary. Even in the sea, after the high tide comes the low tide. Everything should be done moderately, according to Taoism.

Full Overflow Dry

Poem Sixteen

Tao should not stick to vanities or bad thoughts. One should keep the serenity, introducing *"Chi"* (Energy) with sincerity.

Whatever happens to the country or even if alarming cases arise, one can supply the Tai Chi ball with *"Chi"* (Energy), joining Sky and Earth, introducing Postnatal Energy.

The daily practice of static Qigong assimilated by training makes one return to the Tai Chi ball, the core of the body and where the soul dwells.

It is the return to the origins, to the root of life and to stillness.

致虛極、守靜篤。

萬物並作、吾以

觀復。夫物芸芸、各復歸其根。

歸根曰靜。是謂復命。復命曰常。

知常曰明。不知常、妄作凶。

知常容。容乃公。公乃王。王乃天。

天乃道。道乃久。沒身不殆。

The constant return to the root makes everything much clearer. Ignorance of this principle generates restlessness and might cause disasters.

Therefore, one should receive the postnatal Energy daily through static Qigong, so one can have balanced and correct thoughts and a sound body. Join Sky and Earth and become "King".

The union between sky and earth, that is, becoming one with nature, is Tao. Tao has existed for long years and shall continue infinitely in time.

The same happens to the body: it will achieve longevity and virtue if one knows Tao and practices static Qigong; likewise, there won't be opportunity for the disease (maleficent energy) to infiltrate, and one will be able to complete their days and elevate the spirit.

"王" – King

The *kanji* "王" means king. The one who governs the country, the ruler of a nation. "All existence" refers to everything that exists on the face of the earth, including man. It is the insects, animals, plants and flowers, birds, minerals, etc.

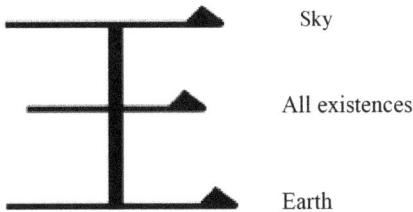

Sky

All existences

Earth

The vertical line "⏽" indicates the union of sky and earth and all beings, obtaining the *kanji* "王". According to Taoism, the King (王) is not only that who governs the country. The true king is the one who, through the practice of static Qigong, keeps his body healthy without maleficent Energy and makes progress spiritually.

In this world, in order to maintain good health and longevity, there is no other way other than the elevation of the soul.

"Tai Chi ball or *Tāi Yuán Xué*"

Just as the plants have roots, our body has its "root", the Tai Chi ball or *Tāi Yuan Xue*. It is a ball which resembles the tennis ball (approximately 8 cm), located 3cm behind the navel and 7 cm in front of the spine.

According to Taoism, the union of sky, man and earth happens at this point, by the practice of static Qigong. So, one returns serenely to the roots without submitting themselves to danger and death, and one leads a healthy and long life.

70

Poem seventeen

The greatest ruler (King, President of the Republic, Prime Minister) is the one of whose existence the people are only aware. Next, there is the ruler who has appreciation for the people and will be greatly praised.

On another level, there is the ruler who governs his country by terrorizing the people, and finally, the one who shows contempt and disdain for the people. In return, the people also despise him. If the ruler does not trust his people, the people cannot trust their ruler.

The ruler should always show magnanimity, always be open to accept any facts, using noble language that commands respect. In addition, he should create an environment in which men can live at ease, naturally.

He should rule in such way that the people would even forget his existence. If the people are successful in an endeavor, the ruler should rejoice and praise them. Every farmer knows the cycle: one plants in the spring, the rain is awaited, then the sun is awaited and the harvest begins.

Therefore, the peasants also live in harmony with nature, as well as the holy masters and wizards of the mountain.

"太" – Thick, a lot

The strokes "大" will be omitted since they were already mentioned. The stroke "、" indicates the Tai Chi.

"人" / *hito* / (Yin/Yang strokes) means that the Tai Chi ball will grow and become bigger.

By practicing static Qigong, the *"Chi"* will be introduced in the Tai Chi Ball, strengthening the root, leading to good health, a long life and elevation of the soul. The thoughts contained here are still valid after more than 2510 years. They will continue to be so from now on. The rulers will need to think long and hard.

Politics is a system in which the more you increase the laws, the smaller will be the freedom, the action and the nature of the people, making them more and more paralyzed. And this is linked to the increased crime rates.

Truly, a good government is "free and natural."

Poem Eighteen

If the great Tao becomes something
obsolete, outdated, the "*Rén*" (benevolent
respect, affection) and "*Yi*" (righteous and
correct act) will come into existence, and
many will become interested in them.
Both "Ren" and "Yi" are artifices that are
not compatible with human nature. If Tao
/ Nature is left aside there will be clever,
greedy and hypocrite men. Father, son and
relatives start fighting because the "xiao"
is required of the child (filial love, respect
and obedience to parents). Also, the fight
happens because the children's parents
and relatives require the "*Cí*" (mercy, love,
benevolence, affection) of them. Parents
should not cover their children with too
much love, benevolence and affection.
Mutual help is necessary but it should not
be exceeded.

六親不和、有孝慈。国家昏乱、有忠臣。大道廢、有仁義。慧智出、有大偽。

A country is disorganized when the free, natural life is taken away from
the people, restraining them with laws. That is why there are subjects who
feign loyalty with words of praise, but think only about the benefits for
themselves. When there is war, military hierarchy arises, and commanders
and soldiers (subordinates) are made avail of loyalty to the superiors.

"仁" – Respect, affection

The strokes "亻" indicate human.

The upper stroke of "二" means Sky or Yang, and the lower one indicates
the Earth or Yin. When the static Qigong is practiced, introducing the Yin-
Yang energies from sky and earth and strengthening the root, the *kanji* "仁"
(rén) will be formed. "仁" in fact means respect to one's self, preserving the
feeling of affection, maintaining health and a long life. Certainly, through
the practice, one will achieve the true "仁".

Taoism advises to live at the mercy of nature, walking through the Great Tao without looking for 仁 (*Rén* – benevolent respect), 義 (*Yi* - justice), 孝 (*Xiào* - obedience or respect for the parents), 慈 (*Ci* - mercy). If one is seeking them, it is because more training is still needed.

Poem Nineteen

The people will live completely happy if there are no clever ones with too much knowledge, who think only about the profits of their immoral sovereign and steal both the freedom and the natural life of men, as well as the clever ones with a talent for intrigues and tricks.

素抱樸、少私寡欲。
三者、以為文不足。故令有所屬。見
民復孝慈。絕巧棄利、盜賊無有。此
絕聖棄智、民利百倍。絕仁棄義、

One should break with the apparent "仁" (*Rén* – benevolent respect) and "義" (*Yi* - justice), which will enable them to rediscover the natural life, and then start to "respect and value parents and relatives." In addition, one will adopt a natural posture that is "慈" (*Cì*- Mercy) "parents loving their children, developing affection and consideration", walking through the path of Tao.

When greed, cleverness aiming profit and intrigues are abandoned, theft is extinguished. The teachings of Tao regarding these actions advise and warn the men who have no virtue.

When one leaves interests and personal ambitions behind, one can live in a natural and free manner, leading a joyful life.

"慈" – Mercy, affection; to love, to value

The left side of " 十十 " indicates Yin and the right one indicates Yang.

" 玄玄" represents " ". The "◯◯" from the upper part indicates Sky/ Yang, the upper part of the human body. And the "◯◯" from the bottom part indicates the Earth/ Yin, the bottom of the human body. The two center points "··" (at the junction of the circles) indicate the Tai Chi ball / *Tai Yuān Xue* / Navel. If one introduces the "*Chi*" into the whole body, one will feel love, and will become a beautiful person with a healthy body and soul.

絶功棄利、盗賊無有

There are no thieves in *Tōgenkyō* (paradise on earth, utopian place). There are (無) no (有) "thieves" (盗賊) where personal interests (利) were abandoned (棄) and the pursuit for success (功) has stopped (絶). Master Lao Tzu says that *Tōgenkyō* (paradise on earth, utopian place) is the ideal world.

小私寡欲

In the words of Master Liu Pai Lin: "Gentlemen, think well. How much is the amount needed for a lifetime? What do you think about doing, accumulating so much money in such a desperate way? Know the limit. Contain personal thoughts and interests. The most important thing is for everyone to know about the "moral", to obey it and to practice static Qigong, introducing the Energy of the Cosmos, leading a healthy and long life. Try to elevate the spirituality, becoming an example to others. Isn't this the main goal for which we were born?"

Poem Twenty

If one interrupts the "studies" one will end the problems, worries and depressions. How much difference is there between "studying" and "not studying"? By knowing Tao and applying it, it is possible to truly live. When seeking diverse knowledge, people bring problems, concerns and greed closer to themselves, and may even fall into depression.

絕學無憂。唯之與阿、相去幾何。善之與惡、相去若何。人之所畏、不可不畏。荒兮其未央哉。眾人熙熙、如享太牢、如春登台。我獨泊兮其未兆、如嬰兒之未孩。儽儽兮若無所歸。眾人皆有餘、而我獨若遺。我愚人之心也哉。沌沌兮。俗人昭昭、我獨昏昏。俗人察察、我獨悶悶。澹兮其若海、飂兮若無止。眾人皆有以、而我獨頑似鄙。我獨異於人、而貴食母。

What is the difference between good and evil? Depending on the person, some thoughts can be classified as good or bad, while others point to another group of thoughts and classify them: "this is good or evil." In the world, one sees a lot of it.

Taoists do not fear what people fear because they have no money or treasures. They do not cause inconvenience to others, nor say words that can hurt people. Why should they fear? Emotional instability, rude or violent acts and speeches are a state of commotion, when the *Chi* is out of the Tai Chi ball, the center of feelings. An advice is to keep the Energy and the feeling contained in the Tai Chi.

"The happy and vivacious people seem to be euphoric, waiting anxiously for the arrival of spring as if they were at a party. But I, all by myself, in a serene and detached state, do not show any of these signs. Just like the baby who has not learned to smile yet, always aimless, as if wishing for nothing. The people are full of desire to be happy, hoarding more and more material goods, but I, alone, have nothing left and I do not wish to leave anything for posterity.

I am in a state of ignorance. Without moving as if I were numb, I am cradled in the lap of the "mother", joining Sky and Earth, because men try to be noticed in their desire to conquer fame, material assets etc., while I prefer to remain as if I were about to fall asleep, without desires and in semi-darkness of consciousness. They all seem efficient and only I seem depressed and listless. Yet, I am like the sea with calm waves, like the waves that float upon the sea and are carried without stopping. They all seem capable and I am the only one stubbornly trying to join Sky and Earth, one inflexible Taoist with a useless attitude. Only for me, differing from all, cradled by the "mother" who is at the same time God, Cosmos, Nature and Tai Chi, to absorb the *"Chi"* is the greatest happiness and preciousness.

"学" – To learn, to study

The three points of "ヽヽノ" indicate respectively "star, sun and moon. "冖" indicates the "lid" of the Cosmos.

The strokes "了" of the *kanji* "子" mean the end, the finalization, while the stroke "➚" indicates the ball (O) = head. "丨" indicates the cervical spine. From top to bottom: head, cervical spine, lumbar spine, sacrum bone and coccyx.

The "一" (number 1) indicates the beginning.

The first animal of the zodiac is the "mouse" (子). It indicates that the zodiac begins. As mentioned earlier, the union of man-woman, Yin-Yang, gives birth to the child (子).

Woman – Yin Man - Yang

Because the stars, the sun, the moon and the Yin-Yang existing in the cosmos come together, one can "learn" (学).

The "alone" mentioned in this chapter refers to master Lao Tzu, and at the same time, the Taoists. One can say that this is a chapter in which there is a detailed reference to the thoughts and way of living of "Tao / the Taoists".

78

"母" – Mother; origin of creation

Complement of poem one.

There are two "mothers" (Yin-Yang). The genitor that gave birth through the union with the father, the mother who raises and nourishes with the existing Yin Energy (breast milk, food) on earth (Yin).

Another mother is "sky/Cosmos". One introduces the Yang Energy existing in sky/Cosmos into the hypophysis (*Lu Pu* - "root" of the spinal cord) through static Qigong. By introducing the postnatal Energy in the Tai Chi ball, the growth with health and longevity is stimulated.

High tide

Full

Low tide

According to Taoism, the human being will not achieve good health, longevity and elevation of the soul if the Yin Energy (Earth) and the Yang Energy (Sky) are not "consumed". Therefore, it is advisable to "assimilate" (学) well the teachings of Tao (道).

For example, if "good" is full and overflows, it becomes "evil". This way, the excess of goodness becomes evil. It's what everyone should know.

Poem Twenty-one

The one who receives the Virtue is the one who unites Sky, man and Earth according to Tao. The principle of Tao is the naturalness without artifice and the absorption. Therefore, one is in a state of ecstasy by focusing one's thoughts only on Tao.

孔德之容、惟道是從。道之為物、惟恍惟惚。惚兮恍兮、其中有象。恍兮惚兮、其中有物。窈兮冥兮、其中有精。其精甚真、其中有信。自古及今、其名不去、以閱眾甫。吾何以知眾甫之狀哉。以此。

Within Tao / Tai Chi / Cosmos there are images and shapes. And within that, there are all the objects. Tao is deep and obscure like the darkness. But inside there is spirit and Energy, the bases for recreating all objects.

That spirit and Energy are the truth that nature created, and one cannot be suspicious of the spirit, the Energy and all the objects which exist in Tao. Since ancient times until the present day and into the future Tao will never disappear.

Therefore, Tao assists and nourishes everything, it corrects laws and destiny, encompassing everything and everyone. The Taoists know about the laws, the fate and about the state of everything in the Cosmos through Tao.

(精) Basic force of life, basis of everything, Energy of the soul

The upper part of the *kanji*, 米, indicates rice. In order to produce rice, Energies of the *Bāguàzhǎng* are necessary. *Bāguàzhǎng* are the 8 natures.

Four Yang Energies >> Sky, lake, fire, thunder

Four Yin Energies >> Wind, water, mountain, earth

The ideogram 精 indicates 8 (*Bāguàzhǎng).*

Next is an explanation about the left part of the *kanji* 精, that is 青. We will separate it in 主 and 月.

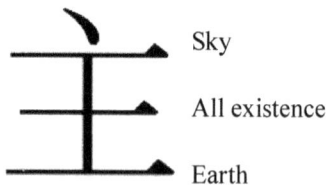

The upper part of "青" indicates "主", Creator, Owner.

From the Cosmos, the Energy from the upper part is introduced, making all existences be born and develop, for example, rice, between Sky and Earth.

"月" (Moon), or "♀" is Yin Energy, meaning water, human body. The dot (·) in the center of "♀" indicates the navel, that is, the Tai Chi ball. Thanks to the "Tao" the production of rice is made possible, like all the other existing things. The "*Tin*" (Essence) and "*Chi*" (Energy) which constitute the sources bring all existences into the world.

"*Tin*" is composed of "Prenatal Energy", a gift received from the parents. This Energy starts to be used more around the age of 15 or 16, and starts to run out around the age of 64. Although, if one introduces "Postnatal Energy" through static Qigong, like the Taoists, one will accumulate the Energies in the Tai Chi ball/ *Tāi Yuán Xué*, generating the children (spermatozoa) of "*Tin*", having vitality even after the age of 100 and enjoying the pleasures of life.

"冥" Darkness, Gloom

It can also mean deep or unclear. As already mentioned, in the cosmos, there are five colors which, mixed in equal quantity, will result in dark gray. This can be confirmed by the colored photo printed on the back of the cover, entitled "... I have glimpsed the sublime. "

「其中有象」「其中有物」

The expressions written in *kanji* above mean: "there is image and shape within this"; "all existences lie within this."

STAR	⟶	WIND
SUN	⟶	FIRE
MOON	⟶	WATER

The "*Tin*" and "*Chi*" are generated with the union of the stars, the sun and the moon, making it possible to recreate all existences. It is the secret of Taoism that is being revealed. One can achieve longevity with the union of the Cosmos, the stars, the sun, the moon, the earth and men.

Poem twenty-two

Some people might think that a crooked tree is not meant for use and therefore they do not cut it to utilize its wood. This way it remains safe. Even so, it will be honored as a "divine tree" when it has lived a thousand years. Whether it is the existence or people's souls, even if they're not perfect in form, they might become so through the laws of Yin - Yang. If there is a cavity, it shall be filled with water.

In the same way, the human being, even if one creates a cavity in the same proportion of the loss of Prenatal Energy existing in the bottom of the Tai Chi ball / *Tāi Yuán Xué*, it will be full of "Prenatal Energy", that is, *Zhen Chi*. Even if there is damage, through the laws of Yin - Yang, it will be repaired. If one studies Tao and practices static Qigong, one will obtain Postnatal Energy. However, if one thinks about being happier and seeks too much knowledge, one will end up getting lost.

曲則全。枉則直。窪則盈。敝則新。少則得。多則惑。是以聖人抱一、為天下式。不自見、故明。不自是、故彰。不自伐、故有功。不自矜、故長。夫唯不爭、故天下莫能与之爭。古之所謂曲則全者、豈虛言哉。誠全而歸之。

Therefore, the sacred master embraces the "one" (一) which equals ○ (zero), because if a circle is cut at a certain point and stretched, it will become "一" (one). The circle (○ = zero) indicates the Tai Chi ball ꙮ, and in turn, Tai Chi refers to the "Mother". Therefore, the sacred master embraces the "mother".

The Taoist practice "*Bào Shù Chūn*" (upright posture, hugging the tree), is one of the representative techniques of this "hug". One holds the Tai Chi – one hugs the mother – and accumulates virtue, becoming an example to others. Since the sacred master does not display his art, people keep thinking about the secret which led him to be so virtuous, only to later discover clearly about his reasons.

The sacred master does not engage in bragging, hence winning the recognition of the people as a virtuous person. He does not propagate his own ability, therefore people praise him in recognition and also, he never discusses or nourishes disagreement, thereupon people never try to involve him in fights.

Since ancient times, the inefficiency of harming people who are not arrogant or dislike disputes is recognized. Would there be any falsehood in this statement?

When fully performing the moral precepts in all sincerity, one comes back to the arms of superb Mother Nature.

"全" Everything, totally

The upper part of the *kanji* "人" indicates the cosmos. The left stroke indicates Yang and the right one, Yin. It is like an umbrella.

It has already been mentioned earlier, but we shall resume the Taoist explanation differently.

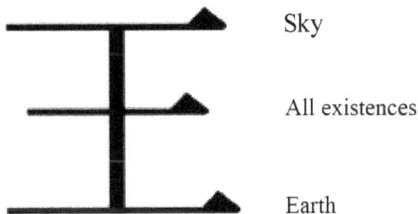

Sky

All existences

Earth

With the union of sky, earth and all existences, the *kanji* for "王" (King) is formed. By uniting sky and earth, gems that are part of all existences are formed.

With the union of sky and earth these precious gems are transformed into beautiful five-colored stones, shining in its "entirety". As was repeated several times, our body is known as small universe and in the Tai Chi ball behind the navel, albeit in a figurative manner, it is said that there are five-colored gemstones.

It is therefore advised to practice static Qigong and let the postnatal energy be in its "plenitude", making the gems glitter in order to achieve "full" health and longevity.

Once unification between sky and earth through Yin-Yang of the Cosmos occurs, all existences are created. This is called "all" (全).

Yin	Yang
Straight	Curved
New (good)	Evil
Few	Plenty
Hesitation (loss)	Obtainment
Short	Long
Existence	Void

"All" is an expression of the theory of Yin-Yang. For example, if something "exists" it will eventually "end". If you "obtain" "plenty", it will eventually be "few" and one will suffer "loss". This is part of the law of nature.

Five-colored precious stones

赤石 red stone

青石 blue stone

黄石 yellow stone

白石 white stone

黒 石 black stone

Poem Twenty - three

Rare pronouncements are natural and contain the truth. But loquacity (habit of talking too much) is interspersed with lies.

The gale which ripples the sea, the hurricane, the storm and the torrential rain that leave their wrath's marks upon the earth do not last long. Almost all of them cease by dawn. Who is the author of all this? It is nature (sky and earth).

If even nature cannot keep its phenomena for a long time, human beings are unlikely to succeed; therefore, those who are dedicated to Tao must study and follow people of virtuous conduct.

信不足焉、有不信焉。

德亦樂得之。同於失者、失亦樂得之。

同於道者、道亦樂得之。

者同於道、德者同於德、失者同於失。

久、而況於人乎。故從事於道者、道

終日。孰為此者。天地。天地尚不能

希言自然。故飄風不終朝、驟雨不

Sinners must open their hearts. The Taoist must think as if it were something referring to himself and solve the cases, leading men to virtue. They must lead those who study Tao with hearts in unison, showing them the beauty of Tao, the joy of understanding nature, and also for all of them to feel happiness and love for obtaining maternal love by practicing static Qigong.

The Taoist should lead those who seek virtue with hearts in unison, so they understand how many joys and wonders the true virtue and the true way of living may bring.

Even for those who have made mistakes or have flaws, Taoists, with hearts in unison, should think of a solution and lead them to goodness. This also causes us pleasure! Performing acts that make others happy! There is nothing more pleasurable than that!

One who has caused others happiness also feels happy with that.

Believe in the "moral". When faith is scarce, one starts to discredit everything that exists in the world. There will be nothing to believe! Nothing causes more unhappiness than that!

The Taoist says: "Believe in Tao" and obtain "*Chi*". Believe in "virtue", learn and become virtuous. Surely, you will feel the joy of living, the tranquility and love for the wonder that life is.

"楽" - Tranquility of body and soul

The center of the top part indicates white (白), the only one that accepts all other colors - yellow, black, blue, red.

In the Cosmos there is the five-color energy and the remaining colors are the result of mixing two or more colors.

As for the two strokes on the sides of "白" (white) "氺" : the top two indicate " sky" and the lower ones indicate " earth".

The *kanji* "木" means tree. The upper strokes "ᐱ" introduce Sky / Yang energy. The bottom strokes "ᐱ" introduce Earth / Yin energy.

"木" (tree) in *tenbun* style, an archaic spelling exemplified beside, in the figure, leads us to the thought that there is nothing that can live longer than a tree.

Since ancient times Taoists have mastered the art of longevity by imitating such form. This technique, already mentioned, is named "*Bào Shù Chūn*", whose detailed explanation is given in the book "Qigong Pai Lin and Chiropractic/ Seitai with Energization" published in 2007.

In a state of "白" (white), the human mind empties, joins sky and earth, captures the energy of the cosmos' five colors, uniting them and obtaining the postnatal energy.

There is no happiness, love or feeling greater than that; I try to share this technique in my books and lectures, so that everyone can reach this stage of plenitude.

"薬" – Remedy

Its lower part is similar to "楽" (tranquility of body and soul, joy).

The left side of the upper part of " ✛ " indicates the Yin energy in the Cosmos, and the right part, the Yang energy.

The stroke "一" indicates that, upon receiving the energies of the five colors of Yin-Yang / " ✛ " from the Cosmos, by leaving the mind empty, one can cure diseases and also prevent them. Thus arose the *kanji* "薬". According to Taoism, practicing the *"Bào Shù Chūn"* (upright posture, hugging the tree) and *"Wu Yun Tou Ti"* (Five-Colored Cloud) techniques, one can prevent "disease" (evil) or cure it. If you still have difficulty in healing, it is recommended to resort to medicinal herbs or phytotherapeutic medicines of temporary or complementary use. Those are "remedies" created by nature. One could say that this is what Taoist wisdom is about.

Poem twenty-four

Those who stay on their toes, forcibly lengthening the spine, or lift their feet up in the air cannot maintain the same posture for too long. If one tries to do something that is above one's own ability it may cause collapse or failure by the lack of a solid foundation. Those who walk with long strides tire midway and can no longer move for having spent too much *Zhen Chi* (prenatal energy).

Unnatural acts make one lose *Zhen Chi* (prenatal energy). There are no enlightened people among those who claim to be educated. Those who claim their acts to be righteous have no logic. Among those who boast of their works, there is no one who has actually achieved success. Those who are really successful do not exalt their achievements.

企者不立。跨者不行。自見者不明。
自是者不彰。自伐者無功。自矜者不
長。其在道也、曰余食贅行。物或惡
之。故有道者不処。

In any era or time, these are immutable truths. Among those who claim to have brilliant minds, there are no brilliant ones. One cannot even think of making them "heads" of any organization.

Analyzing it from the Taoist point of view, they are no different from those who eat too much, who leave leftovers and have superfluous expenses. This type of attitude and behavior, of hoarding things beyond necessary, consists in maleficent acts.

Therefore, those who aim to find the essence of Tao should not have such attitudes.

"功" - excellent, worthy of praise

The upper part of "工", i.e., the stroke "-" indicates sky/ Yang. And the lower stroke "➛" indicates the Earth/Yin. The stroke is facing upwards because it is an allusion to the seeds or seedlings that grow and bear fruit. By combining the two strokes 工, sky and earth are joined together, which makes field products develop. Another meaning of this stroke is the one of going back to sky. The other part of the kanji, i.e., "力" (strength, ability, and power) indicates the strength of *Chi* ⌀. The Yang energy is directed towards the land, uniting sky and earth, and the Yin-Yang effect makes it possible to reap the crops. This means the accomplishment of the true "功".

企者不立。誇者不行

From the Taoist point of view, those who stand on tiptoes and act hastily to make themselves noticed, or those who stride to achieve their goal are just people who do not have sufficient serenity and cannot obtain the "virtue". Walk with focus, thinking of nothing, with feet and Tai Chi ball firmly targeted towards land.

The same goes for life. It is advisable to walk taking one step at a time, calmly, "tiger style". The Tiger walks calmly, except when it is after the prey. The tiger has been respected since ancient times as an animal that is able to obtain large amounts of Yang Energy. In recent times, due to poaching, it is an animal on the verge of extinction.

The tiger is respected by Taoists to a point of being equal to the dragon in importance.

It is advisable to introduce the energy of the earth (Yin) by walking calmly as not to lose prenatal energy. If one walks on tiptoes, flustered or with long strides, one will make the introduction of Yin through the center of the soles impossible. The Taoist walking technique of "*Bù Háng Gong*" promotes the absorption of this beneficial energy.

Put the tongue on the palate, eyes half closed and palms towards the ground. Let the body be totally relaxed. Walk slowly and naturally as a tiger and think of "nothing ". It is ideal to practice in the morning, when Yang energy predominates.

When walking in a place like a park, always try to do it clockwise. That way you will receive nature's "postnatal energy" and the "*Chi*" from the trees. The longer the walk, the more you receive "postnatal energy". Generally, people exercise close to the trees. According to Taoism, the trees/ nature emanate the "*Chi*" in the morning, but steal it in the afternoon. The practice described above is recommended, therefore, in the morning.

Poem twenty - five

Before sky and earth arose, there was something that had undergone mutation. It was something silent, formless and melancholic. Something independent and that no longer transforms itself. Something that is present in all existences and never ceases. It is, therefore, the Cosmos/ Tai Chi and at the same time, mother of all existences.

有物混成、先天地生。寂兮寥兮。
独立不改、周行而不殆。可以為天下
母。吾不知其名。字之曰道。強為之
名曰大。大曰逝。逝曰遠。遠曰反。
故道大。天大。地大。人亦大。域中
有四大。而人居其一焉。人法地地、
法天天、法道道、法自然。

Neither the Taoists nor I (Lao Tzu) know its existence. Thus, we call it Tao. Since the Path (Tao) is immense and deep, we shall name it "大" (great). Because this great thing infinitely recedes, it is called "Shi" (逝 = remoteness, distance, death).

If the state of "shì" is to continue, we call it incomparably "yuan" (遠= far away, distant). If "yuan" continues infinitely, one returns = "fan" (反る). Therefore, Tao (path) is something great (大). Even sky and earth that emerged from Tao are great (大), and man (人) is also great.

In this world, there are four greatnesses: Tao, Sky, Earth and man. The man lives on Earth following the laws of the land. Sky is in accordance with its own laws. Tao is in accordance with Tao, so Tao is natural and therefore in accordance with nature. Man can become one with Tao. Therefore, man is extraordinary. I (Lao Tzu) assemble the four greatnesses. I assemble them in accordance with nature.

"吾" –Oneself, I

In the *kanji* "五", the top part of "吾" means number five, in deep relation to the Yin-Yang theory of the five elements. The five elements of Yin-Yang join sky and earth.

According to Taoist medicine, the center of the navel contains the Tai Chi ball. In case you feel any pain when pressing your thumb towards the Tai Chi ball, it is a sign of a problem in the stomach or in the spleen. Pain when pressing 4 cm above the navel is a sign of a heart problem or one in the small intestine. 4 cm below, kidney or bladder problems. 4 cm to the left, liver or gallbladder. 4 cm to the right, problems with the lungs or large intestine.

Master Liu Pai Lin always examined his patients through palpation. The accuracy of palpation can be compared to that of technology used in current medicine.

The bottom, "口" indicates the small universe (the human body). Man is part of one (一) of the 4 greatnesses in this world. The "一" (means number 1) is 口 → ○ and when cutting and stretching the circle you get "一". Therefore, man can become one body with Tao. For this reason, man is "extraordinary." If man does not introduce the "*Chi*" (energy) from sky and earth into his body, he cannot be great (大). He will be but a simple mammal. One introduces into "吾" (the "I") the 5 (五) energies of the cosmos and the "I" (吾) becomes extraordinary.

Shì (逝), Yuan (遠), Fan (反):

Origin - detachment (distance - Shi) - distant (far - Yuan) - return (back to origins - Fan). Tao, the Cosmos, the Tai Chi, nature and the mother are great and eternal.

Poem twenty - six

Heavy things are, for example, the foot of the mountain where the trees, light things, are rooted, like the sovereign. The sovereign is the root of the people and it is necessary that he becomes their model. Tranquility (靜) is the sovereign of dynamism (動) and agitation (騷). One cannot disturb the heart with intense physical activity or, for instance, with sumptuous feasts and parties.

輕則失本、躁則失君。
然。奈何万乘之主、而以身輕天下。
終日行不離輜重。雖有荣観、燕処超
重為軽根、静為躁君。是以聖人、

Tranquility, indeed, is the sovereign of agitation. Therewith the Master retains, until the last days of his life, the precious treasure that is the prenatal energy (*Zhen Chi*), never being apart from it, living in its fullness the tranquility and stillness, undisturbed by any concerns. He always keeps the usual emotional balance even if beholding beautiful scenery or beautiful precious objects.

Therefore, a great ruler needs to show himself as an example of a "virtuous man", remaining undisturbed and silent as an imposing mountain, without being seduced by glories. Never be a sovereign despised by the people. If the sovereign acts, behaves or governs frivolously he shall lose the nation. If he causes problems or meaningless riots against the people and acts irrationally, he shall lose his good reputation as a sovereign.

"聖" - Person respected for the high degree of Tao and Virtue

The *kanji* for ear (耳) existing at the top left of the *kanji* "聖" is derived from "𦣻" The central internal ones indicate: Yang (superior, Sky) and Yin (inferior, ground) - one can hear the sound of sky and earth through the ear (耳).

The point between the nose and the upper lip is called *Rén Zhong* in Taoist medicine.

The ears, eyes and nose above *Rén Zhong* are the entrances of Yang energy. The mouth (口), which is below *Rén Zhong is* the entrance of Yin energy.

The ears, eyes and nose require two holes to obtain the cosmos'/sky's Yang energy.

The mouth obtains the Yin energy from the earth. The Yin energy comes from the things that are on earth: vegetables, cereals, fruits, fish, meat etc.

Because one obtains the Yang energy through the ears (耳), eyes and nose, as well as the Yin Energy through the mouth (口), one makes a healthy small universe (human body), becoming "king" (王) and in turn, "Sacred Master" (聖人).

The ideogram meaning sacred "聖" is formed by the composition of "耳 (ear) + 口 (mouth) + 王 (King)."

Stillness/ Turbulence/ Root/ Foothill/ Tree

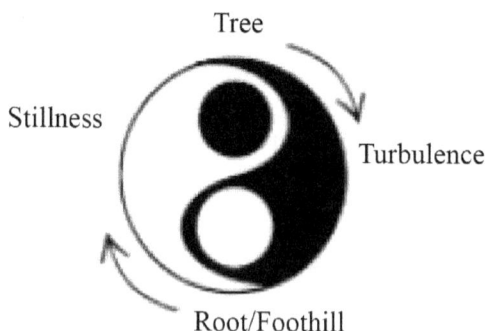

Poem twenty - seven

People who live lives guided by good behavior and good hearts do not leave traces. People who act naturally and with good speech coming from the heart are not misinterpreted. In order to maintain a natural posture, schemes are not necessary.

One cannot open something that has naturally shut itself even if using ingenious tools. For example, one cannot undo a knot tied by a natural phenomenon, like the knot of a vine.

Therefore, the sacred master always teaches about Tao, saves the people and does not abandon them. Likewise, he uses all objects carefully, wasting nothing. All existing things are works of "Tao/the mother." All existences are reborn, transform and develop by necessity. Thus, there is nothing useless.

師、不愛其資。雖智大迷。是謂要妙。

之師、不善人者、善人之資、不貴其

棄物。是謂襲明。故善人者、不善人

善救人。故無棄人。常善救物。故無

結無繩約、而不可解。是以聖人、常

用籌策。善閉無關楗、而不可開。善

善行無轍迹。善言無瑕讁。善数不

In Taoism, this fact is called "clarity" (明). The clarity (明) is the power of seeing everything as God. Therefore, good people, the Taoists and the wise are excellent masters who become role models for the non-virtuous. These, in turn, are the resource for masters to form good people.

However, those who do not respect neither show due courtesy towards the good people who were once their masters do not progress. Likewise, the ones who do not give affection to those yet incomplete who are the fundament to form good people.

All human beings, good or bad, are parts of the same existence created by "Tao/ the mother". The bad people become good with love and effort from the good ones and also because of the teachings of Tao.

If one does not understand this fact, even the wise and educated end up lost in darkness. Taoists consider this delicate teaching to be important and essential.

"明" - Ability to see everything

"日" "☉" indicates the sun and the Yang energy.

"月", " ♪ " indicates the moon and the Yin energy.

With the natural powers of the sun (Yang) and the moon (Yin) one becomes "clear" (明).

If one practices static Qigong and makes prenatal energy full *(Zhen Chi)*, the ability to see increases naturally.

"善" - Good, in accordance with moral

The left side of "➘ ➚" is Yin and the right side, Yang.

The three strokes "三" are: sky, man and earth. Or also, sky, all existences and Earth.

The strokes "业" denote the union of sky, man, earth, and because of the introduction of energy through the mouth (口 =○), one becomes a "good person"

Good  Bad

Poem twenty - eight

When knowing well the instincts and the true masculine nature (Yang) and protecting the instincts and the true feminine nature (Yin), the root/Tai Chi ball of male/Yang and female/Yin is formed. If one practices static Qigong and enhances it with the knowledge of the Yin – Yang origin, one can always be with Tao and the virtue, achieving a natural state without any artifice, like a baby, going back to one's roots. Those who wish to know about Tao have the newborn as an example.

He who has an understanding of the instinct and the true nature of the black/Yin, knowing beforehand about the instinct and the true nature of the white/Yang, will be the example for the people. By becoming an example, one shall be able to return to the world of "extreme void" like a baby, joining sky and earth.

He who knows the glory and preserves the relative shame becomes a source of Yin - Yang. Being a source of Yin – Yang, one shall never lose virtue, that is, one shall always have a full "*Chi*" and can return to the void with the extreme simplicity of a baby that possesses no evil, By dispersing the "Chi", one loses the state of extreme void and becomes a recipient/ Tai Chi ball with no prenatal energy *(Zhen Chi)*.

The Sacred Master, using that recipient - Tai Chi ball - shall become an example by filling it with prenatal energy *(Zhen Chi)*. Therefore, ruling and controlling in a broad manner means to give birth to and transform all existences naturally, as does "Tao/ the Mother". The best way to live is by joining sky, man and earth naturally.

"知" – To obtain knowledge, to perceive

"丿" Indicates the precipitation of "*Chi*" (energy) from the Cosmos/ sky towards the earth.

The upper stroke of "二" indicates Sky and the one below, the earth: the left stroke "人" indicates Yang and the right one, Yin. The right part of the *kanji* "知", that is, "口", indicates the small universe that is the human body.

One introduces the "*Chi*" (energy) from the Cosmos into the body, feeling it and learning to perceive it (知).

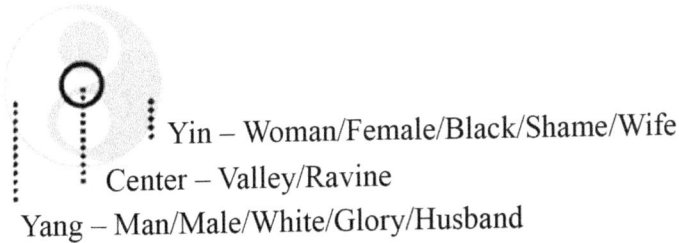

Yin – Woman/Female/Black/Shame/Wife

Center – Valley/Ravine

Yang – Man/Male/White/Glory/Husband

The Tai Chi symbols of ancient times are mentioned in the image beside. The circle "O" in the center indicates the central part of the Cosmos. The top of " ◢ " indicates Yang and the bottom, Yin - indicative of the Earth.

According to Taoism, Tao/God created the cosmos and the stars. Then Tao created the sun (Yang) and the moon (Yin). Then the earth with Yin-Yang

In the human body, the circle "O" indicates the Tai Chi ball behind the navel. This point is the "valley." Water flows from the "valley" with the dynamics of the nature of Yang (sky and mountain top) and Yin (land and foothills). At the same time, the Yin-Yang energy flows through the body from the Tai Chi ball.

"Couple"

If the husband (man/ male) knows his true characteristics and instincts and the wife (woman/ female) preserves her true instincts and characteristics, the couple shall forever obtain a wonderful "happiness" which is the "perfect harmony."

Poem twenty-nine

One has never seen a fool who could perpetuate his deed, forcibly conquered through war, in order to subdue "the country and its people". The universe is a relic created by Tao/God. This relic is something mystic that cannot be reached by the capacity of man. Fools who resort to war, in the end, are defeated and shall become extinct. He who clings to something will for sure eventually lose it. Look at the history of the universe. All are defeated in the end and end up losing their conquests.

将欲取天下而為之、吾見其不得己。
天下神器。不可為也。為者敗之、執
者失之。故物或行或隨、或歔或吹、
或強或羸、或載或隳。
是以聖人、去
甚、法奢、去泰。

All existences spin without stopping even for one single minute. Some things "go" ahead, and others "follow" them. Or, if there is one who aspirates, there is another who expels. If there is a "strong", there will be a "weak". If there is "putting", there will be "draining". The good folk who study the transformations born from Yin - Yang and Tao need to know this: In everything, there are two poles that oppose and complement each other. The two poles refer to Yin and Yang. Because of that, the sacred master joins sky and earth, constantly living in harmony with nature, without practicing remarkable acts, without superfluous spending on clothing, food and housing and never displaying arrogance or pride.

"泰" - Tranquility, calm

The same *kanji* is also used to mean too much arrogance. The Master Lao Tzu decided to use this one and he included the *kanji* "泰"

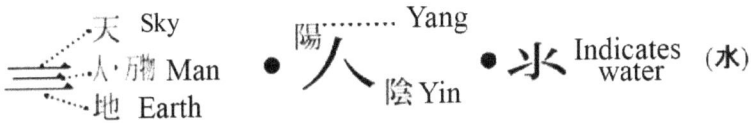

天 Sky
人・万物 Man
地 Earth

陽 ⋯⋯ Yang
人
陰 Yin

水 Indicates water (水)

Because there is unity between sky, man (including all existences) and earth through Yin-Yang, water (rain) precipitates from the sky. Water turns to steam and goes back to sky. With this eternal cycle of "*Chi*" (energy), men and all existences move, are reborn, and thereby become "peaceful".

Theory of the relativity between Yin-Yang

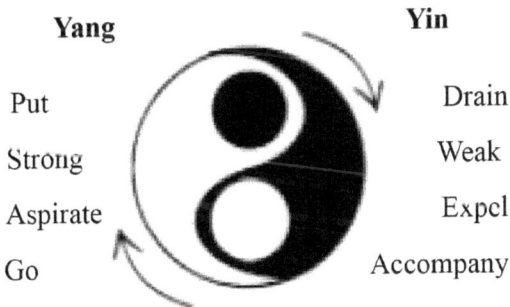

Yang
Yin

Put
Strong
Aspirate
Go

Drain
Weak
Expel
Accompany

Poem Thirty

He who helps the king with the knowledge of Tao does not try to strengthen their country through military repression. If one practices repression, making use of force, he will be subsequently targeted by some misfortune and receive retaliations. The land where armies establish is arid, thorny plants grow and weeds spread.

Whenever war involves the whole country, as a result, years of poor harvest follow, for the farmers are recruited for war and abandon planting.

A good king tries to protect his country by fighting with courage, but never tries to take other countries by force. Even if he fights bravely and succeeds, he never boasts about it. When necessary, he fights with courage, but he always strives so that his people can live in peace. Rigidity brings decrepitude. About this, one says "outrage that diverts from Tao".

If one acts in an unnatural manner, contrary to Tao, he shall find destruction prematurely.

"主" – Owner; Landlord

Man joins sky and earth and becomes king (王). If you put a stroke "、" above the *kanji* for King (王) you will have the *kanji* "主". This kanji indicates the owner, the king, the sovereign, the Father in Sky, the Creator. The religious name it Creator. Taoism is not a religion. One lives by learning from nature, loving it, and unifying it. One respects Tao, the Cosmos, nature, the mother and God.

Poem thirty - one

Taoism and Taoists consider powerful weapons and soldiers to be evil. Therefore, the Taoists are not among them.

It is common for those who occupy higher hierarchical positions to have high regard for the left side, but during war, to prefer the right side. Since weapons of war bring misfortunes, they are not instruments for those who occupy important positions. When the use of weapons is inevitable, one does not attack the opponents more than necessary. Even if one wins the war, it is no virtue.

之、言以喪礼処之。
凶事尚右。偏将軍居左、上将軍居右。
則不可以得志於天下矣。吉事尚左、
而美之者、是楽殺人。夫楽殺人者、
不得已而用之、恬淡為上。勝而不美。
貴右。兵者不祥之器、非君子之器。
有道者不処。君子居則貴左、用兵則
夫佳兵者不祥之器、物或悪之。故
戦勝以喪礼処之。
殺人之衆、以哀悲泣

Only those who kill for pleasure consider such feat as a virtue. Therefore, those who try to find pleasure by wounding and killing their peers will never be able to conquer a country.

In festivities, the left side is the most noble and in funerals the right side is respected. But in the Army, the vice general sits on the left and the high commander (general) sits on the right. Therefore, the army follows the ceremony of a funeral. As the soldiers injure and kill, they must mourn and pray for the souls of the dead, even if they win the war.

"勝" – To win, to defeat the enemy

The Moon (月) is Yin, the human body is Yin –therefore, the Moon indicates the human body. The point "⽉" indicates the navel, the upper section indicates the upper half of the body and below it, the lower half of the body. The left point of " ⟍　⟋ " indicates Yin, and the right one, Yang. The upper stroke of "二" indicates sky and the lower one, the earth, and

"人" indicates man. The last part of the *kanji* "勝", that is, "力" (strength) indicates the precipitation of the Energy "力" from the Cosmos.

One can "win" with the energy of the Cosmos that invades our body and eliminates maleficent energies.

Poem thirty - two

Tao (Path) has no name and is indefinite, like something that cannot be distinguished. It is simple and true. Expressing it in a more understandable way, one can say that it is the "Void", "O".

Tao makes Yin-Yang energies rise, creating all existences. However small, a small object or a human being, the king (world) will not be able to overpower them or subdue them, for all existences created by Tao are independent. If a king knows Tao well and follows its teachings, the people and all existing beings will admire him naturally. Sky and earth unite and dew and rain precipitate from sky towards the earth, immaculate. The energies flow and circulate. If it happens that way, the people shall live peacefully, even if there are no laws.

道常無名樸。雖小、天下莫能臣也。
侯王若能守之、萬物將自賓。天地相
合、以降甘露、民莫之令而自均。始
制有名。名亦既有、夫亦將知止。知
止所以下殆。譬道之在天下、猶川谷
之於江海。

Tao creates all existences and the names appear. The fact of having a name means that they are organic beings. By being organic beings, one day they cease to exist. And again they arise and are extinguished. For example, think of "man." Birth - Baby - Young man - adult - elder - back to sky. He is born from Tao and returns to Tao/ "Yin-Yang", which never cease. All existences are with Tao and return to Tao. This resembles the river which is born in the mountains, runs through the valleys and reaches the immense sea.

"海" – Sea, Ocean

⺡ = シ. Indicates from top to bottom, "Sky," "Man / All existences / Star / Water" and "Earth".

"⼀" Indicates the man = Yang and Yin. " 毋 " - Indicates mother.

Sky, all existences and earth will unite and the Yin-Yang energies will gather and form a huge Sea. It is called "great mother-earth/ sea as great as the mother."

以降 甘露

Dew and rain fall from sky towards earth. Due to the natural dynamics of the sky (sun) they become steam and return to sky. The part that symbolizes the sea "✔" indicates the return from earth to the sky.

知 止 所以 不治

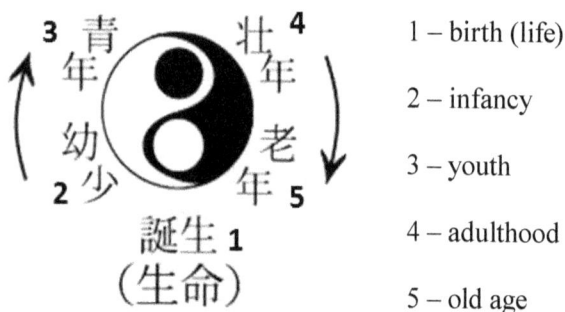

1 – birth (life)

2 – infancy

3 – youth

4 – adulthood

5 – old age

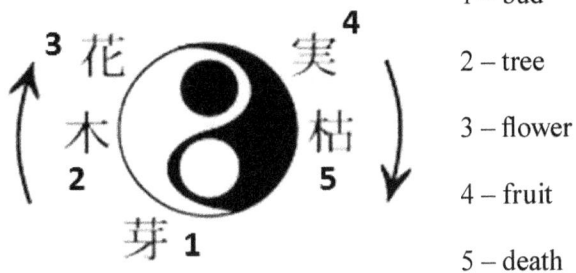

3 花
木
2
芽 1
4 実
枯
5

1 – bud

2 – tree

3 – flower

4 – fruit

5 – death

The Yin-Yang energies circulate on and on, eternally.

Poem thirty - three

People who know their peers well are smart; one can even say that he who knows himself has wisdom.

The sacred master who knows Tao is wise; those who manage to overcome their opponents can be considered qualified, but those who manage to overcome themselves possess true strength.

Knowing the amount that is enough for oneself, not spending too much to cover oneself in luxury, is vital in order to possess spiritual richness. Those who know how to hold themselves back, joining sky and earth, seeking the Path and the Virtue, are those with willpower. Those who follow the teachings of Tao and do not lose their

reason can achieve longevity.

不失其所者久。死而不亡者壽。

自勝者強。知足者富。強行者有志。

知人者智、自知者明。勝人者有力、

The human body is "Yin" and the soul/ spirit is "Yang". Even though the body perishes, those who have conquered Tao shall have their souls immortalized.

"壽" – Merry circumstances; longevity

"三" denotes sky, man and earth; "丿" means unity of sky, man and earth with the Yang energy. "寸" is the small Yin. For an insignificant amount of time.

When capturing the energy by joining sky and earth, one feels happy - a blessed happiness; by practicing static Qigong daily one conquers longevity (長 "壽").

「死 而不 亡者 寿」

The (physical) body is "Yin" and the soul/ spirit is "Yang". At the time of birth, the human soul enters the material body through the hypophysis and settles in the Tai Chi ball located behind the navel. When the body perishes, it is buried and returns to earth. However, the soul leaves the body through the hypophysis and returns to sky. This is why it is said: "Although one dies, the soul is immortal." Parents/ ancestors too, even though they no longer have a material body, they have souls that still live and protect their children. The Taoist advises to take good care of one's ancestors. Master Lao Tzu says the same.

The wise Taoists who are devoted to Tao have Master Lao Tzu's protection even after his death.

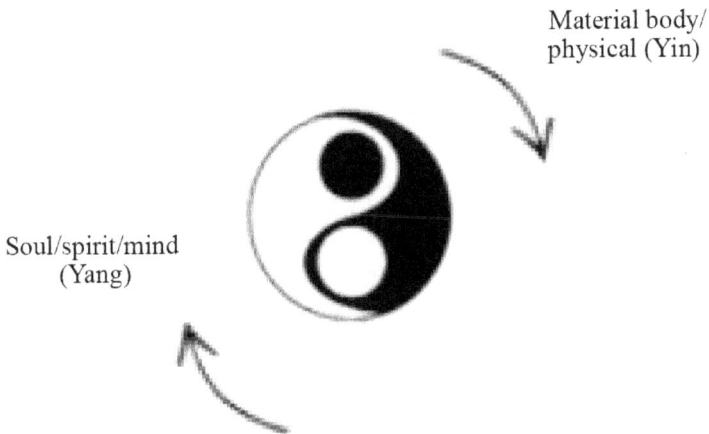

Material body/ physical (Yin)

Soul/spirit/mind (Yang)

Poem thirty - four

"Tao (Path) and the Yin-Yang energies" are everywhere: up, down, left and right. All existences depend on "Tao and Yin-Yang".

However, even creating all existences, Tao does not want recognition.

Moreover, even though it promotes the formation of existing things, it does not try to be sovereign. It may be called "small" because it never nurtures any ambition.

"Tao and Yin-Yang" make all existences develop and also return to their original state.

Therefore, they may be entitled "large".

However, be Tao "large" or "small", regardless of these facts, it completes its movements of Yin-Yang naturally.

Therefore, Tao can make itself "great."

大道汎兮、其可左右。万物恃之而
生而不辞。功成不名有。衣養万物而
不為主。常無欲、可名於小。万物帰
焉而不為主、可名為大。以其終不自
為大、故能成其大。

"左 · 右" – Left · Right

The stroke "一" of the *kanji* "左" indicates Cosmos. The stroke "ノ" indicates that the energy is coming down from sky to earth. And "工" indicates the joining of sky and earth.

The meanings of the strokes "一" and "ノ" in the *kanji* "右" are the same as above. "口" indicates the small universe, all existences and the human beings. Tao fills all existing beings, above, below, to the left and to the right with *Chi* (energy).

112

Poem thirty - five

If one governs the country following the teachings of Tao, one shall not be struck by any damage and the world will know peace.

Travelers walking down the street will stop to listen to the delightful music and smell the pleasant aroma of delicacies that hangs in the air. However, hearing about Tao will sound like a dull story. Even if one fixes one's gaze, one cannot see. Even if one sharpens one's ears, one cannot hear. However, in seeking Tao, one shall never be worn out.

"平" – Plan

The strokes "二" represent: upper stroke - sky and lower stroke, the earth. "丶丿" represent: the left point Yin, and the right one, Yang.

The line "|": from sky to earth and to the underground, it extends infinitely. For example, from the "flat" place (平) the trees, vegetables (tubers), etc. go increasingly deep into the underground.

With the power of nature, of sky, earth and Yin-Yang, trees and vegetables grow properly and in a balanced way, without tilting only to the left or the right.

「用之不可既」

"用" – To use

"冂" indicates ⌒ / Cosmos.

The strokes "二" are sky and earth, respectively.

"|" Indicates growth from top to bottom.

The usage (用) of the Cosmos, of sky-earth and of Yin-Yang has infinite functions.

The Sacred Master and the Taoist have their "hearing, sight and taste" enhanced by practicing static Qigong. Especially the "taste". It emerges as saliva, but there is nothing tastier! It is a taste of diluted honey.

As for the sight, while practicing static Qigong, one begins to see the *"Chi"* (energy), colors and luminosity. The wonderful feeling one experiments at that moment is indescribable.

Master Lao Tzu teaches us that Tao does an endless work and is the pure expression of truth.

Poem thirty - six

If one wants something to "shrink", one should "stretch it" for a while. If one wants something to "weaken" one must first strengthen it. If one wants to "terminate" it for a while, one should make it "prosper". If one wants to "take away", one should "give". It is called the laws of Yin-Yang.

Flexibility and weakness can overcome rigidity and strength. The fish cannot slip out of the river's depths. A country cannot subdue its people by threatening them with weapons. Find the best solution to each challenge, knowing the laws of Yin-Yang / Tao.

将欲歙之、必固張之。将欲弱之、
必固強之。将欲廢之、必固興之。柔弱将
欲奪之、必固与之。是謂微明。
勝剛強。魚不可脱於淵。国之利器、
不可以示人。

"固" – strong, resilient

"口" indicates the cosmos, that is, "O". "十" means the number 10. It means infinite. According to Taoism, there are 10 *"Chi"* on sky and 12 *"Chi"* on earth. "口" indicates small universe / man / all existences.

The human beings introduces the 10 infinite *"Chi"* from the Cosmos into their body and they build a strong physique.

"微 明" - delicate, subtle, precious

Master Lao Tzu used the *kanji* "明" to write "微 明 " when it is usually written with the *kanji*" 妙 ", that is, " 微妙 ". "明" is Yin-Yang. It is believed that the Master used the *kanji* "明" in order to make the laws of Yin-Yang known.

The meaning of "柔弱勝剛強"

Translation: "water is stronger than rock."

Yin = to shrink/to weaken/to extinguish/to give/soft (weak)

Yang = to stretch/to strengthen/to prosper/to strive/hard (strong)

  As strong as one may be, when the peak is reached one becomes "Weak". The Taoists and master Lao Tzu advise to understand the laws of Yin-Yang in order to comprehend the topic better.

Poem thirty - seven

Tao remains always natural and never practices acts that require human hands. If a king rules following moral precepts, the people will then be guided and lead towards good. But the people who did not receive the correct guidance from Tao, even if educated, will see the growth of desire and may resort to artifices. That kind of desire must be cut at the root, and Tao and the state of detachment must be sincerely reinforced. If one divulges the virtues of Tao (Path) with humility, for sure, the people will practice the act of detachment. If people maintain serenity and live in a natural way, there will be a peaceful nation.

不欲以靜、天下將自定。

無名之樸。無名之樸、夫亦將無欲。

万物將自化。化而欲作、吾将鎮之以

道常無為而無不為。侯王若能守之、

"化"- To transform

"亻" indicates the man and Yin & Yang. The point "丿" in "匕" indicates the energy which precipitates from sky towards the earth. "乚" – the energy precipitates from sky to earth, and finally back up (sky), "⌐". The Yang Energy manages to make its "Energy" rush from sky to earth and from earth to sky in a cycle that integrates the laws of Nature.

Man becomes healthy by capturing the Yin-Yang Energies of the Cosmos and expelling evil.

Poem thirty - eight

Those who incorporate the "superior virtue" following the teachings of Tao and practicing static Qigong, like the Sacred Master and the Taoist, do not boast of the skills of "virtue." Ordinary people do not master these skills, because those who dominate the superior virtue live to the mercy of nature and do not act with the intention of being virtuous.

There are people with "lower virtue" who cannot master the superior one, because they acquire it without studying the virtues of Tao and without practicing static Qigong

華
。
故
去
彼
取
此
。

丈
夫
處
其
厚
不
居
其
薄
、
處
其
實
不
居
其

前
識
者
、
道
之
華
、
而
愚
之
始
。
是
以
大

礼
。
失
礼
者
、
忠
信
之
薄
、
而
乱
之
首
。

失
德
而
後
仁
。
失
仁
而
後
義
。
失
義
而
後

応
、
則
攘
臂
而
扔
之
。
故
失
道
而
後
德
。

上
義
為
之
而
有
以
為
。
上
礼
為
之
而
莫
之

為
之
而
有
以
為
。
上
仁
為
之
而
無
以
為
。

是
以
無
德
。
上
德
無
為
而
無
以
為
、
下
德

上
德
不
德
、
是
以
有
德
。
下
德
不
失
德
、

The masters who dominate the "benevolent respect" with certainty distribute love and affection to the people in a natural attitude. They may know that the excess of benevolent respect becomes disrespectful.

The people who possess superior justice, logically, look for the righteous path and act accordingly, but end up feeling that they are above the rest. Taoists limit the sense of "justice" to a minimum.

There are people who have good manners and act correctly according to social etiquette, but if others do not act the same way, they force them to do so.

Thus, when Tao is lost the virtue arises. When the virtue is lost, then comes the benevolent respect. After the benevolent respect is lost, justice emerges. When justice is lost, good manners come. They are nothing but forced acts in order to make subjects devote allegiance to their sovereign. They are frivolous acts and the beginning of chaos.

The Sacred Master and the Taoists who dominate the virtue live naturally, never taking frivolous attitudes and acting frivolously.

They assimilate the superior and true virtue without falsehoods. Therefore, the Sacred Master and Taoists follow the teachings of Tao with firm purpose, ignoring the "benevolent respect, justice and social labels", practicing only the "Taoist virtue."

"德" – To master the teachings of Tao, personality of high moral precepts; Virtue

The upper stroke of "彳" or "丁" indicates sky, and the lower one indicates the earth. The Energies of Sky (Yang) and the ones of Earth (Yin) extend all the way down.

"十" indicates that there are 10 Energies in sky. (十 = 10). It is also what is called "jikkan" (十 干). "Chi" (energy) is infinite and indicates the expansion to 10 different directions.

"囗" Indicates the number four. In nature there are four important elements without which all existences would be unable to be transformed. Also, there is the meaning of 4 sides.

Sky
天 ☰
火 ☲ Fire
水 ☵ Water
地 ☷
Earth

"心" (lower right part of the kanji 德) means heart (true feeling), soul. With sky, earth, fire and water existing in the Cosmos, and the heart in Tao, all existences will grow with luxuriance, reaching the superior "virtue".

Poem thirty - nine

Tao was reached in ancient times. Sky became clear, the land became peaceful, the spirit became active, the valley became filled with water (Yin energy) coming from the earth, all existences mutated, and the king was able to rule. The root of it all lies in Tao. So, if sky had not reached Tao, it would have been torn and would not be able to keep itself clear. The earth would have disintegrated and would not be able to maintain itself peacefully. The spirit would have disappeared and the waters of the valley would have dried up and there would have been no living being. If all existences had not reached Tao,

昔之得一者。天得一以清、地得一以寧、神得一以靈、谷得一以盈、萬物得一以生、侯王得一以為天下貞。其致之、一也。天無以清將恐裂。地無以寧將恐發。神無以靈將恐歇。谷無以盈將恐竭。萬物無以生將恐滅。侯王無以貞將恐蹶。故貴以賤為本、高以下為基。是以侯王自謂孤寡不穀。此非以賤為本邪。非乎。故致數輿無輿。不欲琭琭如玉、珞珞如石。

they would not reproduce and would eventually die. The king would lose his power and the country would be devastated.

In Tao there is Yin - Yang - complementary opposites. Therefore, the "noble one" maintains its existence supported by the "humble one". The low is the foundation of the high: for the peak of the mountain to exist, for example, there must be the foot of the mountain. Therefore, kings and sovereigns should think of themselves as if they were, such as orphans, people who have not accumulated virtue, people who do not work and those that do not practice beneficial acts. Therefore, they should not be treated as a nuisance just because they are from an inferior social position.

Even if one wants many treasures, in the end everything will become "Mu" (nothing , empty) .Even if one accumulates great wealth or lives surrounded by luxury, the decay will come due to the laws of Yin - Yang .

Do not be a distinguished man only on the outside. Among those who dress well and are covered with jewels, there are no worthy men. Reach Tao, assimilate the virtue and become an individual whose heart and Tai Chi ball shine like jewels

"靈" – soul, spirit

"雨" means rain (雨). "⌒" Indicates the Cosmos, the lid, and "⌒" indicates sky. "卜" Indicates the passage of energy from the Cosmos through the clouds.

"卜" and "ː ː" indicate the falling rain. However, as in this case it is "靈" (soul) it means the existence of many souls in sky. "口 口 口" Three souls and small universes – it indicates that they exist in a large number. "巫" - The upper part indicates sky, the lower one, the earth, with the central stroke uniting sky and earth."人" (man) indicates Yin-Yang. "巫" (maiden who serves God) –means daughter of God, in the service of God.

Life 生

Soul 靈

In conclusion, there is Tao, God, Sky and the soul that suffer mutations at a given time.

"Noble and humble, high and low, peak and foothills"

On the mountain, there is the peak because there are the foothills. The country exists as a nation because of the people who cultivate the field (foothills) or work in the city that is why there is the sovereign (peak). The sovereign must be the example of a life guided by Tao; otherwise the country will certainly decay.

Additional explanations of the meaning of "一" (1): This is a circle, but indicates Tao: circle, zero, void, nothing, Cosmos, mother. If one cuts the circle and stretches it, one gets the "一". It is the number 1. Taoism calls it "zero/Ichi (one). Thus, "一" means Tao.

Tao = mother of all existences.

Tao radiates the Yin and Yang Energies and can transform all existences. Men transform and develop when they believe in the existence of Tao and "Yin-Yang", and when they seek "virtue" and obtain the "Chi" (energy). So says Lao Tzu.

High 頂
Peak 上
高
Humble
貴
Noble 賤
Low Foot 下 · 麓

Poem Forty

The "return" movement is the law of circulation of the Energy of Tao. Tao moves in a tenuous and serene way. All things created by Tao are formed by "existences". "Existence" is Yang, and at the same time, it is everything. The existence is born from the "void". The "void" is Yin, and at the same time, it is extinction.

反者道之動。
弱者道之用。
天下萬
物生於有、
有生於無。

"反" - Yin and Yang are opposite

"厂" - "⌒" Cosmos. "又" was formed by the strokes "⺀" being the upper one Yang, and the lower one, Yin. With the existence of the Cosmos and the law of the circulation of Yin and Yang energies, constant inversion (反) occurs.

"Existence, void, opposition"

The existence indicates spring and summer. The void indicates autumn and winter. Most living organisms (insects, animals, birds, plants, flowers) become more active with the arrival of spring, because it is the beginning of Yang. The dynamics of Yang gives birth to baby animals that develop, and then come fall and winter.

Summer
Existence

Fall
Void

夏「有」春

秋「無」冬

Spring
Flourish

Winter
Sleepness

Poem forty - one

If a highly qualified individual hears about Tao, they will follow its teachings and will practice Qigong. If an individual who is proud to be intelligent hears about Tao, they will doubt its existence and soon will forget it. If a fool hears about Tao, he will laugh. If it is not laughed at, you cannot say that it is Tao. The Taoists say: Tao will not be of great value if falsely intelligent and foolish people easily understand it. That is why there are many sayings.

The Taoist who has clear knowledge of Tao, by seeming unconcerned, is seen as a fool. By following the teachings of Tao and constantly developing virtue, one seems to be doing nothing, and perhaps for this reason, one is not as respected as one should be.

Taoists are seen as people without ups and downs. But in reality, every day they join sky and earth. The practice demands great effort and the Sacred Master, as the Taoists, faces thorny paths.

The man who has assimilated the Virtue well, such as a Taoist, is humble and affable. He is as silent as the valley and he is vivacious. He lives naturally and without artifices, he is detached and at first glance, he may seem idle or downhearted, but any magnanimous individual who has achieved the Virtue, by acting calmly and naturally, gives the impression that they are denying something. With the knowledge of virtues and moral, many people wonder: Does this person really wish to live?

A simple and unostentatious man who has obtained virtues seems to live differently than the ordinary people.

Being too deep, Tao has no edges. Being too large, it does not seem to be a perfect container. Huge and deep, although it makes a great noise, it is not heard. Being giant, it has no form, it cannot be seen or perceived physically. Therefore, there is no way to name it. Tao only assists and donates energies (Yin and Yang) to all beings, making them develop and transform themselves.

"上 · 中 · 下"
Superior / Middle / Inferior or Above / Middle / Below

The "中" indicates the Cosmos "○". With a stroke in the middle it is "|". If it is on the horizontal direction, it is as shown by the figure. The upper stroke is "上" (superior, above) and the lower one is "下" (inferior, below). On top of the circle "上" there are sky and Yang. The stroke "|" indicates Yang energy from the center to sky. "—" indicates all existences that develop and transform themselves.

"下" - below the center, there are earth and Yin. "|" - falls increasingly towards earth attracted by the Yin energy. "﹨" indicates the agricultural and mining production.

All of them together mean that all existences evolve and transform themselves.

Poem forty - two

Tao is zero: "empty, zero, sky, Cosmos".
If one cut this "○" and stretches it, it turns
into "一" (1). Therefore, Tao generated the
"一" (One), "one" generated "Yin-Yang"
(Two), and Two (二) generated Three
(三) with the union of Yin-Yang. "3 (三)"
mutated and created all existences, which
in turn received the Yin Energy, and
embraced the Yang energy arising from
the union of Yin-Yang.

Men dislike being orphans, insignificant
individuals without virtue. The sovereigns
and noble men take these features upon
themselves, because they know the Yin-
Yang theory of Tao, that is, there is a cycle
of evil → good →evil. →good. Therefore,
if there are any losses, they become gains
and when the gains are full they become
losses. Tao teaches us: stubbornness,
greed, pride, vanity and avariciousness only lead us to an undignified
death. This teaching is the voice of Sky.

道生一、一生二、二生三、三生萬
物。
萬物負陰而抱陽、沖気以為和。
人之所惡、唯孤寡不穀、而王公以為
称。
故物或損之而益、或益之而損。
人之所教、我亦教之。
強梁者不得其
死。
吾將以為教父。

"二・三" –Two ・ Three

The Tai Chi symbol encompasses both Yin and Yang. The Yang energy
occupies one third of the area of Yin and Yin occupies one third of the area
of the Yang energy. Remember this ratio well. It is correct for the small
circles to be inside the Tai Chi ball ● ○ with the size of one-third of the
bigger circle. It is part of Taoist teachings. There are many misconceptions
in books that deal with this topic.

The Yin Energy refers to 陰氣 (Yin Chi) and also to "things" (matter).
Therefore, the "things" receive Yin Energy in their body, they embrace
Yang Energy, unite and suffer mutation, becoming 三 (3) and creating all
existences. The Yang Energy also embraces Yin Energy.

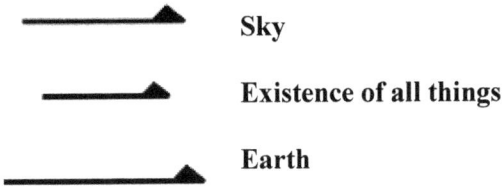

Sky

Existence of all things

Earth

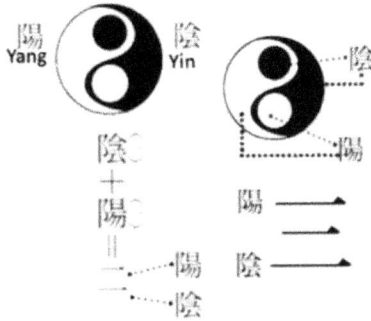

"父" - Father; genitor

The point on the left of "ノ丶" indicates Yang and the one on the right, Yin. The strokes "乂" are thicker in the beginning and become thinner in the end. The stroke that starts on the right and leans into the left is Yang. And the stroke that starts on the left and leans into the right is Yin. Thus, the existing Yin-Yang in the Cosmos precipitate upon the earth, making the "父" (father, genitor) exist. In a broader context, "父" (father, genitor) is Yang and "母" (mother, genitor) is Yin.

Good and evil, gain and loss

Because of its nature, if good is full it becomes evil. If the gain is full, it becomes loss.

Poem forty - three

There is nothing more tenuous than *"Chi"* (energy) in outer space. Nevertheless, it manages to infiltrate even in the hardest organic bodies that exist. Because it has no form, *"Chi"* penetrates everywhere no matter how small the place is.

Therefore, one can understand that the natural way of living, in harmony with nature, preached by Tao, is the most salutary; Tao says nothing. However, how profitable it is to live naturally, without artifices and practicing Qigong. That is what is most valuable in the world!

言之教、無為之益、天下希及之。 有入無間。吾是以知無為之有益。 天下之至柔、馳騁天下之至堅。 不 無

"益" - Increase; useful, fruitful

"丷ㄥ" - Indicates the existence of Yin-Yang energies in the Cosmos. "ノ丶" - Indicates the precipitation of Yin-Yang Energy from the Cosmos upon the earth.

"皿" - Means a shallow, flat container. With the union of Yin-Yang Energies,all existences on earth are transformed and with that, the "advantage" will come (益).

堅 Hard — Soft 柔

Master Lao Tzu says that the "soft" destroys and dominates the "Hard". In this chapter, there is no reference to "water," but one knows that "water breaks the rock." *"Chi* and water,"* which are softer, break the harder things. What is hard one day softens.

Poem forty - four

When comparing the reputation and the body, which one is the most important? Between the body and fortune, which one is more worthy? Comparing the gain and loss, which one causes more suffering? Therefore, by coveting eagerly such things as name, property, and other things, one wastes the "Prenatal Energy" that one has. When hoarding in large quantities, large quantities are also lost, and at the same time one loses their own Prenatal Energy/ *Zhen Chi*. He who does not desire beyond what is required will not be humiliated. If one knows the limit, there will be no danger and one will not lose too much "Prenatal Energy". The *"Chi"* is lost when the threshold of greed is crossed.

知足不辱、知止不殆、可以長久。

甚愛必大費、多藏必厚亡。

名与身孰親。身与貨孰多。得与亡

孰病。是故

Following the teachings of Tao and practicing Qigong guarantee a healthy body and long life.

"病" - Disease, maleficent energy

The upper side of "丷" indicates sky / the upper body and the lower side indicates earth / the lower body.

"广" »» "冖" indicates the Cosmos - the "lid", in this case, indicates the top of Cosmos. "丙" "丙" and "一" indicate the top of the body. "人" indicates Yin-Yang / inside / internal organs.

Maleficent Energy enters the body and causes disease.

"Obtainment / Loss" and "Storing / Disappearing"

Everything that is stored in exaggeration ends up getting lost. Even among people of high position, like doctors, kings, university professors, prime ministers, presidents of large companies, highly qualified people, they rarely live more than 100 years. Greed for reputation, social position and material goods concentrates all the energy at these points and causes the loss of "Prenatal Energy/*Zhen Chi*".

Store | Disapear
Obtain | Lose

2510 years have passed since "The Book of the Path and the Virtue" was written. But since those days, many people have desired to live a long life, and only the Sacred Master and the Taoists who have followed the teachings of Tao and practiced Qigong have reached longevity with good physical and mental health.

Chinese master Zhāng Zi Yang's Proverbs

1. Do not look for a long path at first; get to the root taking one step at a time.

2. Even when it comes to those who claim to be qualified, one cannot know for sure if they are really qualified individuals.

3. A 100-year time is also as fleeting spark.

4. The entire lifetime of a man is like a bubble.

5. Those who seek only wealth and glory do not realize that are wearing themselves out physically and mentally.

6. Ask in which mountain the gold is hidden.

7. Gold is not something you buy easily at any time. Gold / *Chi* is located at the bottom of the navel, in the Tai Chi ball.

According to Taoism, Master Chang Zi Yang had a long life (206 years B.C. 200 A.D.). He is a Taoist from the 北 派 lineage from North 金丹 派 and from *Jin Dan* lineage, well known and respected.

Poem forty - five

Those who have mastered the teachings of Tao seem to be vague, useless people, but actually, through their way of living, their actions and words, they become ideal role models. Taoists whose bodies are filled with *"Chi"* have a vague appearance, but they have an unbeatable mood and are never out of balance. People see Taoists who possess an integrity of body and mind as if their lifestyle, acts and speeches were tortuous. Taoists who can achieve their goals with skills seem infantile in the eyes of the people. True and sincere speech is not understood.

The dynamic Qigong warms what is cold and the static Qigong "cools" the fever. Practicing static Qigong with a pure soul, abstracting oneself, this is the harmony of this world.

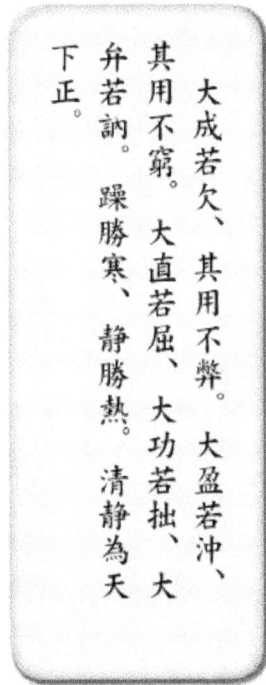

大成若欠、其用不弊。大盈若沖、
其用不窮。大直若屈、大功若拙、大
辯若訥。躁勝寒、静勝熱。清静為天
下正。

"正" - Correct, right

The upper stroke of "工" indicates sky, the lower indicates the earth: and the stroke in the middle indicates the union of sky and earth. Both the vertical stroke and the horizontal one on "丨⁻" indicate the Cosmos - a representation of all things of the universe circulating and coexisting in harmony (正).

Something becomes static when the dynamic is full. It becomes cold when heat (hot) reaches its maximum degree. Energizing practices can be done with the static and dynamic Qigong. The practice of dynamic Qigong is best known as Tai Chi Chuan. The movement promotes the capture of "postnatal energy" from the cosmos which, in union with the "Prenatal Energy", eliminates the cold and expels the evil energy, keeping the body healthy.

Dynamic　　　Static

動　　　　静

熱　　　　寒
　　　　（冷）

Hot　　　　Cold

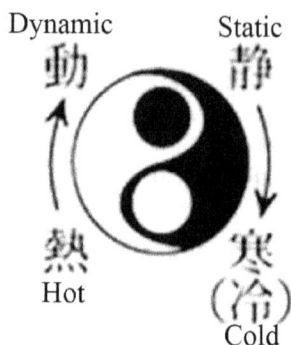

In static Qigong, we adopt the meditation "Sitting on the quiet". The "postnatal Energy" of the Cosmos, attached to the "Prenatal Energy" existing in the body lowers the false fever, thereby cooling the body. This way, one can be in a state of serenity and purity of soul, filling the body with "*Chi*".

Poem forty-six

If countries followed the teachings of the Tao, there would not be conflicts. There would be no need for horses that could be used to plow the fields.

When Tao is forgotten, the war begins and horses are needed to serve in the armed forces.

There is no greater crime than allowing greed.

No bigger doom than an errant king with no limits to his satisfaction.

There is no greater immorality than eagerly trying to get everything you want.

足常足矣。
於不知足、
戎馬生於郊。
天下有道、卻走馬以糞、天下無道、
罪莫大於可欲、禍莫大
咎莫大於欲得。
故知足之

So restraining yourself means to limit ambitions to a minimum and to want nothing more than what is necessary.

If one knows the righteousness and how to restrain oneself, the morality arises, and by practicing static Qigong, longevity is reached.

"有" – To exist

" 亠 " / " 大 " Indicates the Cosmos, location from where the Yang Energy " 冖 " precipitates in a downward trajectory " 丿 " "月" indicates the shape. The energy which comes from the Cosmos originates (makes, 有) the organic substances, that is, all the existences.

Taoism recommends not to be greedy, to preserve the body by capturing "Energy", to live a long and healthy life and to try to elevate spirituality. It is also recommended that Taoists offer guidance on "Virtues", Qigong and the natural lifestyle, receiving the "love of the second mother" (Cosmos) and distributing love for the people. This is the true "love."

Poem forty - seven

The Sacred Master knows the social situation of his country, the politics, the life and thoughts of the sovereign and the people without leaving his home.

Even without watching the sky from his window, he knows the Energy and the movements which govern the laws of nature.

If one searches for wisdom on the streets of the city, or with any other means, without focusing on studying the path and the virtue, without practicing static Qigong, man will increasingly distance himself from Tao, decreasing moral knowledge.

其出弥遠、其知弥少。是以聖人不行

不出戶、知天下、不闚牖、見天道。

而知、不見而名、不為而成。

Consequently, the Sacred Master knows the true way of living, understanding and predicting without seeing or hearing, and, acting by doing nothing, he is able to achieve his purpose.

"出" – The act of leaving; arising

The strokes " 屮 " indicate the outbreak of the bud.

"丨" - Sky (Yang) introduces the Energy on Earth (Yin), by uniting sky and earth comes the bud.

The Sacred Master lives in the middle of a mountainside and hardly ever goes to town. This place is perfect to capture the Yang from sky and Yin from earth.

Everything can be seen while practicing static Qigong. Tao and virtue arise.

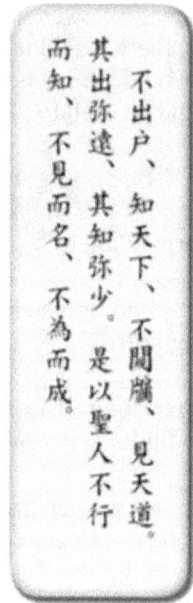

Poem forty - eight

The more one studies, the more one knows. But there is a limit of information that we can store without exhausting our brains.

If one practices Qigong and follows the teachings of Tao, the artificial and meaningless knowledge will decrease.

When it decreases to a maximum, one reaches a state of absorption and freedom. If one reaches the natural world with serenity, one will be able to act freely, annulling oneself.

A king or sovereign should, whenever possible, allow his people to act freely, wishing for them to live without disease and without misfortunes.

常以無事。 及其有事、 不足以取天下。

以至於無為。 無為而無不為。 取天下

為学日益、 為道日損。 損之又損、

The more a king makes use of artifices, the more respect from his people is lost, and he will find it difficult to rule.

"不" - Term of denial

"一" indicates the earth.

"个" Indicates the underground or subsoil. The organic substances existing below, on the right and on the left, will not arise. There will be no harvest or minerals. The things that exist in the underground (Yin) will not emerge or grow.

A king should not restrain the people with laws and regulations. He should let them be free, as much as possible, so that they may live and prosper in a natural environment.

Master Lao Tzu says that the lifestyle of the indigenous is part of one of the utopias. In Japan, this refers to the Ainu people.

Who destroyed the free lifestyle?

Poem forty – nine

The Sacred Master is always empty-minded and serene-spirited. That is why he can read the hearts of the people as if they were his own. What the people believe it is good, he also considers good. Even if it is evil, he considers it good. Both good and evil are balanced in Yin - Yang, with no major differences. This is called good virtue.

What can be trusted, he considers reliable. What cannot be trusted he also considers reliable.

Likewise, reliable and unreliable are balanced in Yin - Yang, with no major differences. This is called good virtue of Tao.

聖人無常心。以百姓心為心。善者
吾善之、不善者吾亦善之。德善。信
者吾信之、不信者吾亦信之。德信。
聖人在天下、歙歙為天下渾其心。百
姓皆注其耳目。聖人皆孩之。

The Sacred Master accepts people with magnanimity, not caring about good and evil, nor about reliable and unreliable. When the Sacred Master utters the words, everyone opens their eyes and ears trying to understand and, as if they were listening to the voice of "Tao / God", they listen as engrossed as an innocent baby .

"信" - Truth, not telling lies

"亻" indicates man (人).

"言" indicates the act of speaking.

"二" (the first two strokes) indicate the Cosmos.

"=" (The last two strokes) indicate sky and earth.

"口" indicates the small universe/man.

Man (small universe/body) can live a life with no lies, with sky and earth/ Yin-Yang that exist in the Cosmos, practicing static Qigong.

One will have a capacity that will firmly establish the noble character, the goodness and the sense of justice. This is called "reliable virtue."

Meaning of "good / evil / belief / disbelief"

The good, being full, becomes evil, and the belief, being full, becomes disbelief. If one calmly explains the teachings of Tao to a nonbeliever, in an easy and understandable way, one can make him a believer.

Poem fifty

Once the Yin energy is extinguished, the Yang energy emerges. Likewise, if the Yin energy runs out, beings are born. If Yang Energy ends, Yin energy arises.

In the same way, if the ultimate moment comes, beings die. If one divides "life" into ten parts, the period of real value is three parts.

If you divide "death" into ten parts, the period of real value is three parts.

The "life" of a man, among the ten efforts, ends after one third of these efforts, which are made in vain.

Why does this happen? Because, against the laws of nature and the cosmos, many seek to live intensely, which causes great loss of Prenatal Energy.

Those, however, who seek to lead life through the Path of Virtue and the practice of static Qigong, will become virtuous people like the Sacred Master and will not face the dangers that external enemies may present.

Even beasts or weapons will not attack them. Why? People who have attained Tao and the Virtue are devoid of greed and do not try to harm others.

Besides, they are people who have an understanding of life and death, and also of Yin and Yang.

"死" - Death, extinction of life

一" indicates the earth.

"夕" indicates the human body.

"ヒ" indicates transformation.

With death, the soul rises to sky and the body is buried, becoming "earth." In the case of human beings, for example, the male ejaculates around the age of 16 (8 + 8 = 16).

Around the age of 64 (8 x 8 = 64), the number of spermatozoa decreases, as well as sexual desire. This happens because at 16, prenatal energy is enhanced, and it reaches its peak around the age of 20.

From there on, it is gradually reduced until the age of 64. The period between 16 and 64 years is called "the period of value of the third part."

According to Taoism, after the age of 64, starts the second spring (life) .歲, /sai / means "years" (old).

According to master Lao Tzu, a worthless life that is led in vain amounts to one third of ten parts.

It means that there are many people who live in vain until they are 64 years old. Master Lao Tzu advises to have a healthy and long life in harmony with sky, earth and nature, assimilating "Tao and the Virtue" in order to have a life truly worth living.

Life and death - one needs to lead the life cycle correctly. Among people who are retired, some still work, while others are dedicated to their hobbies.

But how many of those are joining sky and the earth, capturing the postnatal Energy and following the teachings of Tao?

How great is the number of people who live a life devoid of value!

Poem fifty-one

Tao generates all existences and the Virtue, nurtures and creates them, forming them and concluding the cycle with the circulation of Yin and Yang. Consequently, all existences respect – or should respect – Tao and worship the Virtue as something valuable. Even worshipping Tao and the Virtue, all existences are born, grow and transform themselves with the circulation of Yin-Yang, always in a natural manner. Therefore, Tao generates and the Virtue nourishes, leading them to full growth.

All existences develop under protection, in such way as not to contract maleficent energies.

恃、長而不宰。是謂玄德。之、蓋之、覆之、生而不有、為而不德畜之、長之、育之、亭之、毒德之貴、夫莫之命而常自然。故道生是以万物、莫不尊道而貴德。道之尊、道生之、德畜之、物形之、勢成之。

Tao and the Virtue generate all existences, but do not take possession, do not seek rewards nor dominate them, albeit making them grow successfully. That is called *"Xuán Dé"* (swift/ghostly virtue).

"常" - constantly, always; unchanging moral

The point on the left of " ﹨ ﹗ ／ " indicates Yin (moon / water), the central point indicates the stars and the wind and the stroke on the right, Yang (Sun, Fire).

" ⌐ " - Indicates the top of the small universe."

" ⊏⊐ " - Indicates the body of the small universe.

" ⊓⊔ " - The Yin and Yang energies circulate eternally from the Cosmos down, providing vigour to the body and all existences.

玄=Ȯ » » 玄 德 (*Xuan Dé*) » » "玄" (*Xuán*). "+" It is like a kind of antenna connected to the Cosmos. The Upper Circle indicates Yang (upper half of the body), and the lower circle indicates Yin (lower half of the body). Man receives Yin - Yang Energies from the Cosmos in his body, eliminating malignant Energy and achieving the "Virtue." By practicing Qigong, he elevates his character, kindness, the sense of justice and personality.

The act of incorporating Tao and the Virtue is called "玄 德" (*Xuan Dé*). The most important thing to learn in "Tao and the Virtue" is "respect ".

Respect to Tao, respect to the Taoist who guides one on Tao and the Virtue. Without feelings of respect, the art of Tao and the Virtue are not mastered.

Poem fifty - two

Tao is the beginning and it becomes the mother of all existences; by knowing this mother, it is possible to know her child. Through the practice of Qigong, it is possible to lead a healthy life until the time of death, receiving all the love, as if curled up in the mother's lap, protecting, respecting and admiring this mother (nature). At the time of death, one returns to the origin, that is, to the mother.

天下有始、以為天下母。
既得其母、
以知其子、既知其子、復守其母、没
身不殆。塞其兌、閉其門、終身不勤。
開其兌、濟其事、終身不救。見小曰
明、守柔曰強。用其光。復歸其明、
無遺身殃。是為習常。

The human body is endowed with five senses. When one blocks these senses, closing one's eyes and the spiritual gate, one dedicates one's attention to the world of the "void" and, wrapped in the arms of the Mother/Nature, one detaches oneself from the outside world. That is, difficulties fade away.

If one opens the entries to the five senses and looks at the wonders of the world, listens to beautiful music, feels the delicious flavors, aromas and perfumes, greed will increase, making one forget about the grace of nature, and one shall never be saved.

The narrow -minded man with little virtue is called, at most, "little enlightened". By devoting oneself to the union with nature, practicing Qigong and introducing *"Chi"* (energy), one will be able to have a strong and resilient body. If one returns to the Yin-Yang energy, using its light and obtaining the *"Chi"*, the body shall never suffer.

Live a long life curled up in the mother's lap, practicing Qigong with "Tao and the Virtue."

"塞" – To Cover; to close

" 宀 " - Indicates the upper part of the Cosmos.

" 卄 " - Indicates all existences.

" ノ 丶 " - Indicates Yin-Yang.

" 土 " - indicates the earth (Yin).

With the upper part of the Cosmos/ lid, all existences are "closed".

"明 / 暗" - Light / dark and "復 帰" – Return

If the "light" is full, it becomes "dark". With time, from the dark one "returns" to light.

The "Five senses" refer to the eyes, tongue (mouth), nose, ears and skin.

What is known as oriental medicine or Chinese medicine has its origins in Taoist medicine.

· Oriental Medicine: Japan, Korea (over 2000 years)

· Chinese Medicine (over 5000 years)

· Taoist Medicine (over 7000 years)

For better use of energy, here is a Taoist secret: during the practice of "static Qigong" the eyes and mouth should be closed.

One puts the tongue on the upper palate and breathes gently through the nose in an almost imperceptible way.

Try to ignore all sounds.

This closes all the senses. By keeping oneself in this state, one introduces the *"Chi"* (energy) of the Cosmos and stores it in the Tai Chi ball located behind the navel.

Poem fifty - three

If there are people with some knowledge of Tao, what is feared is that they stray from the main path - which is flat, wide and easy to follow. Nevertheless, people like shortcuts, although these may not have a way out.

It would be best to walk along the main path, but greed leads them to search for something better. The shortcuts, as one advances, become narrower until there is finally no way out.

When the Imperial court is sumptuous, the tendency is to think that politics is taking place in an unbiased manner. Quite the contrary: the fields are abandoned and people's pantries are empty. Men in court dress luxuriously, carry excellent swords, stuff themselves in lavish banquets and have plenty of goods and treasures. We call this big thief who does not fear God.

也哉。厭飲食、財貨有餘。是謂盜夸。非道

畏。大道甚夷、而民好径。朝甚除、田甚蕪、倉甚虛。服文綵、帶利劍、

使我介然有知、行於大道、唯施是

"介" – To help, to assist, to aid

" 人 " - Indicates Yin-Yang and is shaped like an umbrella.

"丿|" - Symbolizes the Yin and Yang energies from sky, "helping" all existences.

Taoism teaches: man must walk the "main path" and have it as a model to be followed. When one walks along the main path, Mother, God, and Tao will lead one towards happiness; if one seeks shortcuts, he shall have no way out and shall end up sick.

Admire a river that reaches the sea, home to the Mother. If a river goes off course and enters the affluents it may find no way out. There is no example of a country that has endured for many years when the king, president, prime minister or the court has committed excesses. Surely, the fall never takes long to come. The ruler should always think, above all else, about the happiness of his people. We call that "the great path".

Poem fifty - four

A good building has a strong structure and does not collapse; similarly, a good body with the Tai Chi ball full of Prenatal Energy repels diseases, as well as maleficent energy.

善建者不拔、善抱者不脱。子孫以
祭祀不輟。修之於身、其德乃真。修
之於家、其德乃余。修之於鄉、其德
乃長。修之於国、其德乃豊。修之於
天下、其德乃普。故以身観身、以家
観家、以鄉観鄉、以国観国、以天下
観天下。吾何以知天下然哉。以此。

Those who hold on to the "energy" firmly will not be out of prenatal energy because they keep the body sound. If they study and assimilate "Tao and the Virtue ", descendants, Taoists and Taoist ceremonies shall never be extinct.

If they master Tao, the Virtue will be real. If family members assimilate Tao, it will be inherited for many generations, and virtue will always be accompanied by happiness.

If a village assimilates Tao, for a long time it shall have a fruitful land. If the nation assimilates Tao, its people will be free and love nature, they will respect their ruler and will have spiritual wealth.

If the world assimilates Tao, it shall be everywhere, creating a world of peace.

Therefore, if everyone studies Tao, the virtue and practices static Qigong one shall see oneself; if the family studies Tao and the Virtue, they will be connected to their origins; if the nation studies Tao and the Virtue, they shall find themselves at peace; if humanity studies Tao and the Virtue and practices them, it shall see the world in peace.

How can one know that the world will be that way? It shall be that way due to the fact of having explained the Way and the Virtue of Tao.

"観" – To see, to contemplate

The " 𠂉 " part of the *kanji*, that is, " 隹 " indicates cosmos/ 𝟛, and " 𠂉 ", the path of the energy from sky to earth.

" 隹 " Indicates all existences. All existences refer to men, birds, insects, plants, minerals etc., everything that has form and image.

The right side of the *kanji*, that is "見" / "𮥸" -the circle indicates cosmos and the inner strokes in the circle indicate sky and earth. "儿" - indicate the Yin-Yang energies.

It means that the Yin-Yang energies from the Cosmos/ Sky come to earth in order to nourish and enlighten, "contemplating" all existences.

It is through this act of "contemplating" the Yin-Yang energies with the practice of static Qigong, with the Virtue based on the teachings of Tao and joining nature, that one obtains true wisdom. What can there be beyond this?

Poem fifty - five

The Taoist with great virtue from Tao can be compared to a baby. Bees, scorpions, vipers and snakes do not bite him. Even beasts do not approach nor do the raptors attack him. That is because babies are innocent, have no greed and are pure of soul.

早　氣　和　至　而　螫　含
己　曰　曰　也　握　猛　德
。　強　常　、　固　獸　之
　　。　、　終　。　不　厚
　　物　知　日　未　據　、
　　壯　常　號　知　、　比
　　則　曰　而　牝　攫　於
　　老　明　不　牡　鳥　赤
　　、　。　嗄　之　不　子
　　謂　益　。　合　搏　。
　　之　生　和　而　。　蜂
　　不　曰　之　峻　骨　蠆
　　道　祥　至　作　弱　虺
　　。　、　也　。　筋　蛇
　　　　心　。　精　柔　不
　　不　使　知　之　而
　　道　　　和

The babies' bones are fragile and its muscles are soft. However, its handshake is firm. And the erection of its genitals occur without any relation to sex. This is because the baby's prenatal energy, born from the union of the father (Yang energy) and the mother (Yin energy) is full and has great vigor. The baby does not go hoarse even if it screams all day. It is because the baby is in communion with sky and earth. It is because the "prenatal energy/ *Zhen Chi*" is active.

Know that the union of man, sky and earth is constant. Know about the "constancy" and introduce "*Chi*" through this union. That is called "*Cháng Ming*" (constant enlightenment). "*Ming*" (enlightenment) means the union of Yin (moon) and Yang (Sun).

Many mundane men think that justice is the same as "taking advantage" in life. Without joining sky and earth, not caring about the withering and loss of "*Chi*" , they act only in order to foster their greed. The more one acts that way, the earlier one ages. This is called "person who has strayed from Tao (Path)". Those who have strayed from it shall never have a long, healthy life and shall not know the elevation of the soul.

"日" - indicates "☉"/ sun

"子" - Indicates "♀"/child/ body/ spinal cord.

In Cosmos there is the Sun and Yang Energies. One introduces the energy into the body, activating and "thickening" the soul and the prenatal energy.

The Taoist advises: return to the baby status. The baby is pure and natural. Breathing is abdominal. One can observe the curling of the baby's abdomen. One of the secrets of longevity is the technique of curling the abdomen (Tai Chi ball) while practicing static Qigong.

Poem fifty - six

Not many are truly wise: those that boast "wisdom" are not. The Taoists and those with a noble spirit close the senses, diminish the sharpness of the heart, appease the anger, dim the bright light and place themselves at the same level of ordinary people. This is called *Xuán* (玄). It is the natural life, without any artifice, the plenitude between sky, man and earth.

Thus, questions arise: should one seek some intimacy or stay away from people of noble spirit or Taoists? Should one consider them as noble or ignoble people? In any case, the important thing is to seek "*Xuán*".

知者不言、言者不知。塞其兑、閉
其門、挫其鋭、解其紛、和其光、同
其塵。是謂玄同。故不可得而親、不
可得而疏。不可得而利、不可得而害。
不可得而貴、不可得而賤。故為天下
貴。

"光" –To shine, to illuminate

" ＼Ｉ／ " – Indicates the brightness of the sun, the moon and the stars.

" ── " - Indicates that one receives on the recipient.

" ﾉﾚ " - Indicates the Yin-Yang that comes from sky and distributes light for all existences. The stroke on the right "ﾚ" is facing up in an upward motion, returning to sky.

Taoists and the noble-spirited are those who live naturally with no artifice, joining sky and earth. Ordinary people speak and advise on matters which they haven't mastered, creating embarrassment and misleading situations.

Thus, the Taoists and people of noble spirit leave everything on nature's account, avoiding to make pronouncements and to explain about the natural course of life.

Poem fifty - seven

One rules a nation at peace with justice and true Tao. When greed increases, one begins to act insolently and it drives the nation to war, resorting to countless soldiers.

In order to rule the country in a peaceful state, it is necessary to adopt a very natural conduct, without artifice.

How do I (Lao Tzu), the holy masters and Taoists know that the best way to govern the country peacefully is the one in harmony with nature? Because of the reasons explained below.

The more rigorous the laws are, the more the people are impoverished, physically and spiritually. The more weapons are developed, more and more bloody struggles follow. The more technology advances, the more people use it to satisfy their greed and become its slave, without knowing that they are wasting the *"Chi"* (energy).

The more new laws emerge, the more numerous and clever the thieves become. Therefore, the sacred master says: "If I give the example of spontaneous action, without any artifices, people will change. If I display serenity, people will return to fair sense by themselves".

By keeping themselves without desires and following Tao and the Virtue, the people shall have spiritual wealth. If each one remains in a state of total self-annulment, the people shall return to spiritual purity by itself.

May sovereigns assimilate "Tao and the Virtue"!

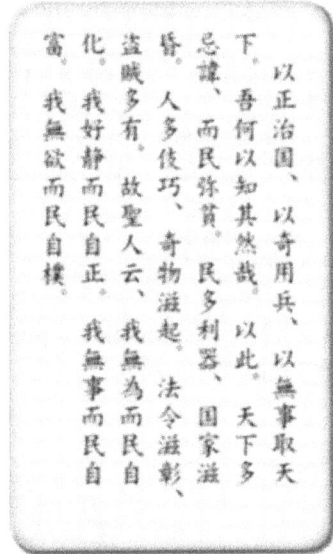

"富" – Abundance

"宀" / "⌒" - Indicates the Cosmos.

"⬚" - Indicates the small universe, the body.

"田" - indicates the farming field, the crop. The farming field is made with *Bāguàzhǎng*: the wind, the water, the mountain and the earth = Yin energy: the sky, the lake, the fire and the thunder = Yang Energy, adding up to eight elements. Our body receives the energies of Yin-Yang from the Cosmos and the Tai Chi ball becomes full.

The solid continuous line represents " ▬ " Yang, and the segmented one "▬ ▬", represents Yin.

The Taoist says: "The products that have usurped the true energy and the true justice are the treasures, weapons and new technologies, among others." From now on, the technological developments in all areas promise to make our lives easier.

It has been over 2500 years since master Lao Tzu left us the Book of the Path and the Virtue, but have the people become spiritually wealthier?

How great is the number of greedy people who lose their true Energy and true justice! How great is also the number of people who flatter others! Therefore, it is natural for them to perish physically and spiritually.

In the XXI century, the rulers are concerned with the preservation of nature, but if they only seek practical solutions, they will have great difficulties. Scientists, technologists and many others could think of a way for humanity to return to nature and to the pure spirit.

And the best way is Tao. What the master Lao Tzu wants to stress in this chapter is: "Return to mother nature." It is true that many people would like to live close to nature, in a nice and quiet environment, so the answer is in this book. Embraced by the mother, receive "postnatal Energy" with the practice of static Qigong.

In the weekends, millions of people travel to the mountains or beaches. Why is that? Is it not because they want to relax, joining nature? One returns to nature with the practice of static Qigong, joining sky and earth, in harmony with nature. Return to the arms of the "Mother"!

154

Poem fifty-eight

When a government adopts laws that are closer to Nature, the people will have spiritual wealth and live in peace. If the government is bad, sanguinary, tyrannical or omissive, its people will live frightened, lost or insecure, not believing in the "system."

Disgrace (Yin) is opposed to happiness (Yang). Each hides the other. If happiness is full, disgrace rises. There is no limit to disgrace or to happiness, like there is no standard to say which of them is correct. Even righteousness can hide a mistake, because good can also become evil.

People do not know these laws that govern the Yin-Yang and therefore, remain in confusion, or succumb to ignorance.

其政悶悶　其民淳淳。其政察察、
其民欠欠。禍兮福之所倚、福兮禍之
所伏。孰知其極。其無正。正復為奇、
善復為妖。人之迷、其日固久。是以
聖人方而不割、廉而不劌、直而不肆、
光而不耀。

Consequently, the Holy Master, having this knowledge, remains righteous and never takes actions that may harm others. Although he is honorable, he does not boast, even if others show themselves bright as deities, the Holy Master does not try to shine; he carries himself simply like someone who dominates the "Path and the Virtue".

"政" - To guide and correct the people, to govern the country

"正" – To correct all Energies of sky and earth, in the vertical and horizontal direction. Balance of Energy.

"攵" / "攴" – The top indicates the Cosmos, the horizontal stroke indicates the reception, and the crossed strokes on the bottom " 乂 " indicate the precipitation of Yin-Yang.

By receiving the Yin-Yang Energies of the Cosmos, a nation is managed correctly. Yin = mistake, evil; Yang = righteousness, good. When happiness reaches plenitude, disgrace happens, and when disgrace ends, happiness rises. If good reaches plenitude, it becomes evil. Yin and Yang are in constant movement.

Yang		Ying
Good		Disgrace
Rightness		Unexpected
Happyness		Curse

"To be hidden" - what is the real meaning?

In the Tai Chi symbol there are two small circles (● / ○) representing, respectively, the fact that within the Yang Energy there is a third of Yin Energy hidden (● = Yin Energy) and within the Yin Energy there is a third Yang Energy hidden (○ = Yang Energy).

Take the "good" as an example: even though it says it is good, inside it there is a third of "evil", because nothing can be considered entirely "good".

The Tai Chi symbol is occasionally represented with the internal circles smaller or inverted. Do not be fooled!

黑 black - in relation to the Yin area, the white 白 – Yang area occupies a third, and vice versa.

黑 白 白 黑

156

Poem fifty-nine

The ruler who governs offering happiness to the people is the one who lives in a simple way, joining nature and respecting Tao.

"To obey Tao and the Virtue" means to accumulate Virtue and follow the teachings of Tao, that is, Tai Chi. To understand Tai Chi means to know and understand the laws that govern Yin-Yang and to know peace.

A nation sheltered by the mother (Tai Chi, Cosmos, nature), will live on forever.

This is, according to Tao, a teaching on how to prosper forevermore.

治人事天、莫若嗇。夫唯嗇、是謂
早服。早服謂之重積德。重積德、則
無不克。無不克、則莫知其極。莫知
其極、可以有國。有國之母、可以長
久。是謂深根、固柢、長生、
久視之
道。

"極" – Extreme, Cosmos

"禾" >> "朿" >> "夫" - means the man imitating the tree.

"叝" >> " " >> " " - Tai Chi ball. It indicates the outermost Cosmos or its end.

The Taoist says: one imitates the tree and obtains the Yin-Yang of the Cosmos and becomes filled with "postnatal Energy".

Poem sixty

The king who rules a large state seeks to maintain the liveliness of the people in a natural way, leaving them at ease without resorting, as much as possible, to the laws, like the cook who prepares a small fish without making it lose its natural taste. When one rules according to the precepts of Tao (Path), one does not need to fear the demons.

To let beings live freely and naturally - this is the true work of God. The true God never hurts man nor allows him to have harmful thoughts. He just tries to let him live naturally. Such as God, the Holy Master also never does anything that might hurt the feelings of man.

治大國、若烹小鮮。以道蒞天下、其鬼不神。非其鬼不神、其神不傷人。非其神不傷人、聖人亦不傷人。夫兩不相傷。故德交歸焉。

Both God and the Holy Master attempt to harmonize nature and man's freedom. The people respect God and the Holy Master, but they are not aware of their existence. That is why they are happy and in peace, loving nature and freedom, complying by Tao and accumulating Virtue. God is nature. Tao is the teaching of nature. Therefore, Tao is "God."

"神" – God

The explanation about those who create and dominate the Cosmos was given earlier, but we will discuss a little more about it.

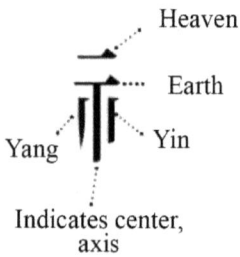

ネ>> "示" - indicates that the Energy (*Chi*) of sky and earth extends in a downward trajectory. The stroke to the left of " ıı " means Yang, and the one in the right means Yin.

Heaven

Earth

Yang

Yin

Indicates center, axis

申>> ✺ - symbolizes *Bāguà* (*Bāguàzhăng*) = Yin - wind / water / mountain / earth; Yang - Sky / lake / fire / thunder.

The upper stroke that crosses ✺ indicates that it is linked to sky. And the lower stroke means it is linked to earth. The Yin-Yang and *Bāguà* (*Baguazhang*), are the nature in Uno, that is, God. This God brings light to all existences.

Poem sixty-one

A large country can be compared to the estuary of a river. It's where the small rivers (countries) run to, and where they mix. In other words, a small country can be compared to the female (woman), who is always silent and beats the male (man) with tranquility. The woman is serene (Yin) and the man is dynamic (Yang). By being dynamic, the man loses more prenatal energy and lives less than the woman. This way, woman beats man.

Therefore, if a large state (compared to the estuary of a river / man) is below a small country (spring of the river/ woman), it can earn its respect. If a small country is below a big country, it will earn its respect.

大国者下流。天下之交。天下之牝。牝常以静勝牡。以静為下。故大国以下小国、則取小国。小国以下大国、則取大国。故或下以取、或下而取。大国不過欲兼畜人、小国不過欲入事人。夫両者各得其所欲。大者宜為下。

A large country wants to protect its land and its people, just as a small country desires peace within their territories, often counting on the protection of a larger neighbor. The wishes of both will be satisfied when they show themselves humble: the large state must be the first to demonstrate humility, because arrogance does not guarantee the respect of small countries. Mutual respect will consolidate peace among the people.

"国" Nation, Country, Territory

"囗" represents the Cosmos.

"王" (king) unites sky (superior), man (middle) and earth (inferior).

Under the great universe, man joins sky and earth, leading the people to peace and the nation to security.

Yin = small country / weak country / spring/ female / woman / wife / serenity.

Yang = great country / strong country / estuary/ male / man / husband / dynamism.

Making an analogy between large and small countries versus woman (wife) and man (husband), we may conclude that a peaceful and secure nation is achieved when everybody is respected. Likewise, a couple manages to maintain a stable and harmonious life by respecting one another at all times.

Women (Yin - Serenity) usually live longer than men (Yang - dynamism) because the internal parts of the female body are Yang, and the external are Yin. Yin envelops Yang. The male body, internally, is the opposite.

Since the man's Yang Energy stays outside the body, he loses it more easily. Therefore, he lives less than the woman.

Poem sixty-two

Tao encompasses all existences, taking the Yin-Yang Energies into the depths. The good ones have it as a treasure, and for fools it represents an "existence" that protects them like a God.

道者萬物之奧。善人之宝、不善人之所保。美言可以市、尊行可以加入。人之不善、何棄之有。故立天子、置三公、雖有拱璧以先駟馬、不如坐進此道。古之所以貴此道者何。不曰以求得、有罪以免邪。故為天下貴。

People cherish the words that impress, and the respectful attitudes are considered good. But why abandon the bad? Tao surrounds everyone with maternal love, whether they are good or bad.

So, where is the need to have a king and ministers, to raise walls and possess many warhorses? When men join sky and earth, obtaining the *"Chi"* (Energy) along with learning the "Path and the Virtue", they will achieve peace.

Why is it that, since ancient times, the Taoists and Sacred Masters venerate Tao?

These men knew that, through the practice of static Qigong in the sitting position and with the orientation of the Taoists on Virtue, they would reach "Tao and the Virtue". And even if they had committed a crime, if they assimilated "Tao and the Virtue", they could be forgiven.

Therefore, Tao is what leads to world peace. It is something precious and nothing surpasses it.

"人 人" These are two kanji, each one meaning "people". It indicates that there is Yin-Yang on both sides.

"⊥" Indicates sky and earth. The Energy of the Cosmos is introduced, uniting sky and earth. Men "sit" to capture the Yin-Yang energy of the Cosmos.

"One sits and follows the path of Tao."

One assimilates Tao and the Virtue through static Qigong, surrendering to the path of Tao. This way, one achieves health and longevity, as well as the elevation of the soul. This is the goal of Tao.

Poem sixty-three

A good life can be guaranteed with the practice of static Qigong, joining sky and earth, following the natural course. In doing so, one will not go through unpleasant situations. If the great is complete, it will become small, if the numerous is complete, it will become few. Being familiar with the laws of Yin-Yang to repay resentment with virtue. Trying to solve the problems so that resentments do not take larger dimensions.

為無為、事無事、味無味。大小多
少、報怨以德。圖難於其易、為大於
其細。天下難事必作於易、天下大事
必作於細。是以聖人終不為大、故能
成其大。夫輕諾必寡信、多易必多難。
是以聖人猶難之。故終無難矣。

The problems of this world start small, until they take gigantic proportions, as well as the great cases, which are architected in the smallest details.

The Holy Master solves any problem before it becomes larger. That is why he can complete a great life. Frivolous people, who are unable to resolve anything, end up losing the trust of others.

If one faces the situations as something that can be easily resolved, for sure, this will become a very difficult problem. That is why the Holy Master takes action in relation to any problem early, not struggling his whole life.

"味" – Taste

It also means to taste through the tongue. To feel and know through experience.

164

" Ц ">> ○ "indicates the small universe (body).

" 十 " >> The upper stroke indicates sky, and the lower one, the earth. This is because the Energy arising from the Cosmos extends to the underground.

" ＞＼ " – The left stroke indicates Yang, and the right one, Yin. They are the foods that are on the earth and underground, such as meat, fish, vegetables, fruit etc. The food is "tasted" through the body and mouth. Life experiences are "tasted". Experiences are "tasted" by practicing static Qigong and Energy (saliva) is "tasted".

"癌" - generic name for malignant tumors

" 厂 " - Represents the Cosmos and " ↘ " Sky and Earth, Yin-Yang.

"品" it is important to mention that in our body - small universe - there are countless tumors. The Taoists knew of the existence of "cancer" for over 7000 years. Repaying resentment with virtue, despite being a difficult practice, is in conformity with the Tao; applying it in your daily life is the shortest way to become a true Taoist.

Poem sixty - four

Moments of peace are easy to maintain; it is simple to take action before problems arise. When these are fragile and in the initial stage, they can be solved easily. However, taking measures before they get evident avoids compromising the order.

Even large trees grow from a tiny bud. Even a nine-story tower is built from the foundations; even a path with a few miles begins when the first step is taken.

其安易持、其未兆易謀、其脆易泮、其微易散。為之於未有、治之於未亂。合抱之木、生於毫末；九層之台、起於累土；千里之行、始於足下。為者敗之、執者失之。是以聖人無為、故無敗；無執、故無失。民之從事、常於幾成而敗之。慎終如始、則無敗事。是以聖人欲不欲、不貴難得之貨；學不學、復眾人之所過、以輔万物之自然、而不敢為。

Those who act contrary to the laws of nature end up failing; so, since the Holy Master lives at the mercy of nature without taking any action, he does not know the word failure. He is not attached and, therefore, has nothing to lose.

Some people end up failing a few steps away from success when they engage in something. Why is that? It is because what was meant to be originally natural becomes artificial with the increase of greed. Acting with humbleness from the beginning leads to successful endeavors.

The Holy Master remains detached and does not value the treasures that people consider valuable. He does not study what the people study, only Tao and the Virtue. He turns to "Nature" and to Tao, which were forgotten by people. Therefore, he only leads beings to peaceful union of Yin-Yang in a natural way. The Holy Master architects nothing, leaving everything at the mercy of nature, in the Mother's arms (Cosmos).

"易" - Divination, easy, simple

"日" "☉" indicates the Sun.

"勿" "☽" indicates the moon.

The sun is Yang and the moon is Yin – one reads fortune through the principle of Yin-Yang, foreseeing the future. One reads the circulation of Energy from the sun and the moon. Through the Energy of Yin-Yang, one has a healthy body with 'easy' moves.

Among living beings, except for men, all live in harmony with nature. Thus, they can complete their life cycle. Man ends up shortening life by increasing greed and becoming artificial.

The "disease" is caused by the person and not because the Illness *Chi* (maleficence) infiltrates the body. That is why the Holy Master keeps himself natural, harmonizing with sky, earth and nature, having a long and healthy life.

Poem sixty - five

Since ancient times, the Taoist that follows Tao is one who does not try to make people become wise, but one who makes them know Tao and the Virtue, joining nature. A country finds it difficult to govern their own people because there are many wise men among them. When one tries to rule through the wise, traitors come up. The country with no wise men is the one that harmonizes with nature and brings happiness to its people. One knows the wise and the Taoists well by observing them, as well as the act of observing Yin-Yang brings understanding of its laws. It is called *Xuán Dé* (fugacious virtue): assimilation of goodness and honor by practicing static Qigong. It differs from all existences. In time, one reaches the stage of "Taoist", joining and submitting oneself to nature.

古之善為道者、非以明民、將以愚
之。民之難治、以其智多。故以智治
国、国之賊。不以智治国、国之禍。
知此両者、亦稽式。常知稽式、是謂
玄德。玄德深矣、遠矣、与物反矣。
然後乃至大順。

"智" – Intelligence

"丿" - indicates "☯" / cosmos / Yin-Yang / Tai Chi.

"天" - the upper stroke indicates sky and the lower one indicates earth.

"口" indicates the small universe, the body.

"田" Indicates the Sun.

The Yin and Yang Energies are introduced into the body, as well as the solar Energy from the universe, activating the hypophysis, hence becoming "knowledge" of the Taoists, who fully know the laws of nature.

When wisdom reaches plenitude, it becomes "stupidity" (愚). If stupidity achieves its maximum degree, "wisdom" sprouts (智).

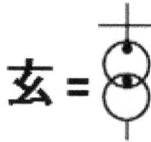

As for the "Xuán Dé", the strokes "十" indicate five Yin Energies and five Yang Energies, adding up to "ten energies". "〇" - The point (·) on the top refers to the hypophysis, the gate which will receive the Energy from sky.

The figure on the right has two circles corresponding to the halves of the human body, whose center is the navel. (·) / Tai Chi, ⊖ and the bottom stroke (|) indicates the *Yīn Qiāo*, the Yin Energy gate. This is one of the Taoists' secrets.

The Yin-Yang energies of sky (hypophysis) and earth (*Yīn Qiāo*) are introduced in order to assimilate Tao and the Virtue, goodness and honor, becoming a complete human being.

To this the name 玄 德 "*Xuán Dé*" is given. Doing nothing and feeling nothing; it is called the "gate of 玄 德 *Xuán Dé*".

This is a Taoist adage.

Poem sixty - six

Large rivers and seas are kings running through the valley, for they lie on lower places.

By noticing this, the Holy Master adheres to the use of language, and demonstrates consideration and affection to lead the people peacefully. He meets all, always in servile position, and, by showing himself humble, people do not feel downtrodden before him.

Although of high character, he does not seek prominence and, therefore, is never attacked.

Thus, if a nation or its leaders put "Tao and the Virtue" into practice, everyone shall live happily and in complete peace.

江海所以能為百谷王者、以其善下之、故能為百谷王。是以欲上民、必以言下之、欲先民、必以身後之。是以聖人、處上而民不重、處前而民不害、是以天下樂推而不厭。以其不爭、故、天下莫能與之爭。

An orderly and peaceful nation, without struggles, shall be built.

"江" – Great River

"氵" - the top spot indicates sky; the second spot, in this case, indicates "River / Great River"; and the last stroke indicates the earth.

"工" - indicates sky / Yang and earth / Yin; water arises when they unite; the rivers originating from the mountains run through the valleys and affluents, and the place where they meet is the "great river".

Countries, social organizations, businesses and families should be that way – that is what master Lao Tzu preaches.

Poem sixty - seven

People have said, for a long time now, that the Tao I preach is foolish. Because of being great, it seems foolish.

But I have got three treasures preserved in my heart, which are: "benevolence" - giving mercy and compassion their true value; "economy", and "humbleness" - not staying ahead of others."

From benevolence emerge courage and love; from economy and appreciation of simplicity, a magnanimous person emerges. Being humble means not to stand ahead of others.

天下皆謂我道大，似不肖。夫唯大，故以不肖，若肖，久矣，其細也夫。我有三寶，持而保之。一曰慈，二曰儉，三曰不敢為天下先。慈，故能勇。儉，故能廣。不敢為天下先，故能成器長。今舍慈且勇，舍儉且廣，舍後且先，死矣。夫慈以戰則勝，以守則固。天將救之，以慈衛之。

And not cultivating, sincerely, these three concepts will cause the extinction of the prenatal Energy, which leads to death. "Benevolence, economy and humbleness" - leading life with these three treasures maintains a sound body.

Tao, the Mother and God will protect the good-hearted, who shall have longevity and love.

"慈" - To love, to cherish, to have compassion

" ⌄⁄ " » " 十十 " indicates Yin and Yang and their union.

" 幺幺 " » " 88 " The upper circles (○) indicate sky/ upper body, and the lower ones indicate earth/ lower half of the body.

"心" » "心" – indicates heart, spirit, soul. By uniting Yin-Yang and by firmly introducing the Energy throughout the entire body, the feelings, the spirit and the benevolent soul are cultivated, offering love to one's own health and to that of others.

"Not staying ahead of others" – Humbleness.

Not imposing one's presence or showing off; when one needs or can actually contribute, one should do it with love. However, one should not stay ahead of others for long: when offering services with "love", do not give too much, for those who receive them end up abusing and becoming incapable.

Poem sixty - eight

A good soldier knows the art of combat. The good warrior does not get angry, nor does he let himself be disturbed, and avoids combat. Whether it is in war or in a common society, one can say the same. Those who can control their men better are the ones who show themselves as humble. This is called the "Virtue of non-combat", which makes the most of human potential. Above this are sky and earth, Yin-Yang and Tai Chi, say the Taoists.

"怒" - Getting angry, upset

"女" indicates woman, Yin energy.

"又" again, once more.

"心", heart, spirit, soul. »» 心 » ψ » 心

When disturbed, women become annoyed (怒) easily.

The Taoists say that the symbol of Tai Chi represents Yang / white (man) and Yin/ black (woman) hugging, for both must help and respect each other!

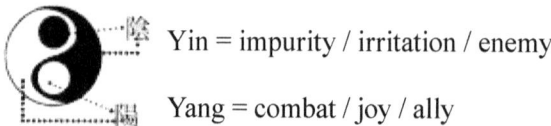

陰 Yin = impurity / irritation / enemy

陽 Yang = combat / joy / ally

Therefore, if an ally reaches plenitude, then the enemy arises. But this poem refers not only to war, but to social order in general.

Poem sixty - nine

I have something to say to the leaders who make use of soldiers: may they not be arrogant but have the same attitude of a guest – in a conflict, do not make the armies advance and, if another country attacks, retreat and defend oneself. Thus, one shall have a peaceful and prosperous nation, for all countries will only conquer happiness by not using weapons. However, when facing enemies with levity, disgrace shall be huge: one shall lose lands and people, who are precious assets. Therefore, when the soldiers' strength is equivalent, the one who replies to the attack first shall win. This is called "Strategy of Virtue".

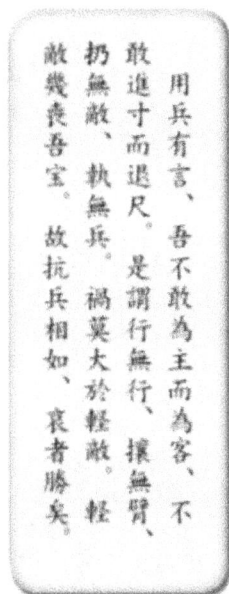

"宝" – Something very precious

"宀" is equivalent to "亼", the upper part of the Cosmos;

"玉" indicates unification. From this union emerge the country, the people and the treasures (valuable goods).

In a full attack, fierce defense shall win, and history proves that, in battles of balanced forces, he who attacks ends up being the loser. God is not ally with the arrogant or greedy.

Advance 進軍・攻撃 Attack

Retreat 退却・守備 Defense

174

Poem seventy

The "Path and the Virtue" that I preach are easy to understand and to implement. However, some are not able to understand or practice it because of a lack of enough information.

Words have a basis and, behind the facts, there is an educated person, with a good and pure character. By failing to understand this fact, some will remain ignorant and foolish. They cannot understand themselves.

Rare are those who know themselves and study, that is, they are precious existences. Therefore, the Holy Master, without covering himself with fine garments, practices the static Qigong, hugs the Tai Chi ball and is wrapped in the arms of the mother, the Cosmos.

是以聖人、被褐懷玉。
是以不我知。知我者希、則我者貴。
莫能行。言有宗、事有君。夫唯無知、
吾言甚易知、甚易行。天下莫能知、

"吾" – Oneself, I

"五" = "𠄡" / "𠀎" indicates five elements.

Elements	Yin	Yang	Colours
Fire	Heart	Small Intestine	Red
Earth	Spleen	Stomach	Yellow
Metal	Lung	Large Intestine	White
Water	Kidneys	Bladder	Black
Wood	Liver	Gall bladder	Blue

"□" is equivalent to "○", representing the small universe, the body. The energies of the five elements are introduced into the body, which is the small universe, and the "I" is "embraced by the mother."

The Five Elements theory of Yin-Yang is part of Tao, the basis and foundation of oriental medicine. Keep them in mind! By capturing the energy of the Cosmos, "I" receive all the treasures.

In this world, the selfish, the proud and the greedy would never have the ability to understand the "Path and the Virtue". It is necessary that they learn from the Taoists.

They shall not be happy even if covered in material goods; only those who learn and practice the "Path and the Virtue" shall obtain true happiness. If Tao could be easily assimilated by man, it would not be as valuable.

Being daily cradled by the mother is what deepens the knowledge. It is actually easy.

Poem seventy - one

One needs to know that there are limits to knowledge.

Disease does not invade the body voluntarily, but it affects those who, while trying to obtain knowledge in an exaggerated manner, compromise the brain cells. If they can understand this thesis they will not become sick.

The Holy Master does not become sick, he knows the limit of knowledge and does nothing to cause the disease. This way, one can have a long life without illnesses.

" 炁 " - *Chi* (Energy)

This *kanji* has the same reading as "氣" (*Chi*), being interpreted only by Taoists.

"二" - Indicates sky and earth;

" ノㄥ " - Represent, respectively, Yang and Yin.

" 灬 " - Is the representation of fire.

Through static and dynamic Qigong, man obtains the postnatal energy; with it, the body heats up, the negative energy is eliminated and a healthy body is built.

According to Taoist teachings, most human beings die at the age of $9 \times 9 = 81$. Even if one lives more than that, the prenatal energy becomes scarce and the body loses its vitality and some movements.

Thus, malignant energy invades the body and man dies.

However, the Holy Master, receiving the *Chi* from the Cosmos, attains longevity.

Poem seventy - two

Subduing the people by fear will not have a good effect; people will lose respect for their rulers and will revolt.

One cannot deprive man of freedom, because then he shall no longer obey the laws that destroy freedom.

In contrast, the Holy Master knows himself well, not showing off with Tao. He preserves his mind, body and spirit through the practice of Qigong and does not flaunt his worth.

He departs from the people and lives in the mountain until he is called by God, in the arms of the Mother (Cosmos).

故　是　無　民
去　以　厭　不
彼　聖　其　畏
取　人　所　威
此　、　生　、
　　自　。　則
　　知　夫　大
　　不　唯　威
　　自　不　至
　　見　厭　。
　　、　、　無
　　自　是　狎
　　愛　以　其
　　不　不　所
　　自　厭　居
　　貴　。　、
　　。

"民" - Components of state society

" Ɛ " Indicates the existence of the Cosmos and the place where the people can live;

" ㇇ " The upper part indicates the Yang energy and the right stroke (﹨) indicates the Yin energy.

The ascending edge indicates the return to sky.

Master Lao Tzu recommended for rulers to instruct their people to live naturally, without imposing rules and laws to them, as much as possible; not finding a natural environment, he went to live in the mountains.

It was there that he obtained the Yin energy from the earth and the Yang energy from sky in a balanced way.

Poema seventy - three

When one takes the initiative and acts with boldness and courage, prenatal energy fades; in other words, life is shortened. He who controls his actions does not lose prenatal energy, therefore, he shall have a longer life. Each positioning has its own benefits and disadvantages. Courage is dynamism, Yang energy. By moving such Energy, man will spread it and be "disadvantaged". Living naturally means serenity (Yin energy). The serene silence, as well as the static Qigong, is an "advantage" because one absorbs energy.

謀天網恢恢、疏而不失。

不言而善応、不召而自来、繟然而善

是以聖人猶難之。天之道不争而善勝、

者或利、或害。天之所悪、孰知其故。

勇於敢則殺、勇於不敢則活。此両

Tao "despises" this courage. Among the people, who shall know this fact?

Even the Holy Master considers it difficult. Winning means obtaining energy. Losing means to spread the energy. Even though one does not enter a dispute, by obeying and staying in the mother's/Tao's arms, he shall win. Even if one does not speak, the body will react well. If one stays in the arms of the mother/ Tao, even if not calling it upon oneself, one shall be surrounded by love and affection received as though from the mother who hugs the newborn.

Sky / Cosmos is infinite, immense, a wide and extensive net of *"Chi"* that makes all existences grow.

"勇" – To face without being intimidated

" 〓 " Is "o" and indicates the small universe; "田" is " ⊕ ", indicating sky, earth, fire and water. It indicates *Bāguàzhǎng*; "力" - is "勹", indicating the strength of the Cosmos and Yin-Yang.

Everything is faced with "courage" through the dynamics of Yang obtained from sky and fire, as well as the dynamics of Yin obtained from earth and water.

Good luck, Yin: naturalness, serenity, obedience, loss.

Bad luck, Yang: courage, dynamism, rebelliousness, victory.

Even if one goes through suffering, famine and unfortunate events, enduring everything in silence, someday happiness will come. When bad luck reaches plenitude, good luck will arise. Reading the chapters 2 and 73, it may seem like Master Lao Tzu contradicts himself, but it is difficult to assimilate his concepts. When one does so, one shall be a true Taoist and feel the reason of living.

Poem seventy – four

If one conducts politics in a fair, righteous manner, the people will not fear death, nor will it be necessary to establish capital punishments. However, bad politics, which is not thought or made for the benefit of the people, is imposed through death penalty. The people are induced to fear death constantly, arresting those who break the law.

The executioner who readily carries out the penalty and plays God, as well as his principals, shall receive Divine punishment. This kind of nation shall not exist for long.

"手" - Hands

" 一 " is " ○ ", the head, the Cosmos.

"二." Superior: shoulder/Sky; Inferior: elbow/Earth.

" 亅 " , the arm. The lower part, bent, indicates the wrist.

The Yin-Yang Energies, as they are received, flow through the blood and nerves, making the hands move freely.

According to Lao Tzu, Tao must be taught to those who have broken the law, so they may regret their actions and be reintegrated to society. It is the foundation of order and peace and must be a reference to the maintenance of a fair and free society.

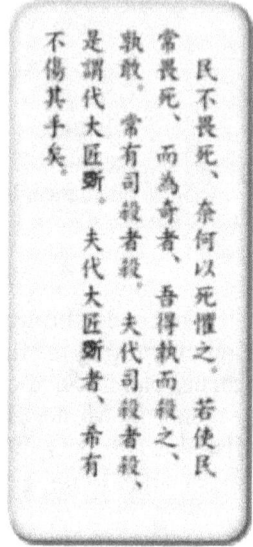

Poem seventy-five

The people suffer with starvation when paying extremely high taxes; it is natural that they should be starving. If it is not possible for the people to live freely and in a carefree way, it might be because there are too many laws to be observed, obeyed, and respected. That way, it is natural for the people to rebel, becoming difficult to be ruled.

If the people do not value life and inevitable facts, such as death, are seen frivolously, it is because the government encourages greed. It is natural, in this case, for the people not to have a long life, to lose their prenatal Energy and not to attain longevity. The government must provide an environment favorable to a free, joyful life.

民之饑、以其上食稅之多。是以饑。

民之難治、以其上之有為。是以難治。

民之輕死、以其上求生之厚。是以輕死。

夫唯無以生為者、是賢於貴生。

The true lifestyle is maintained more often for the people who have a high degree of wisdom than for the ones who belong to high hierarchy or have high positions.

"貴" - Excellent, valuable, important

" 虫 " >> " ◗ ": the left half indicates Yang and the right half indicates Yin. One cuts in half with "I".

"一" – indicates sky, head, Cosmos.

"貝" = "合": the circle indicates the small universe; the upper stroke on the inside indicates Sky and the upper half of the body; the lower stroke indicates the earth and the lower half of the body.

"ノ丶" – Indicate the Yin-Yang Energies.

The Yin-Yang Energies are captured from the Cosmos through the hypophysis and circulate through the whole body (small Universe), making it healthy. It is recommended that the human being, receiver of this life in this world, studies Tao, becoming noble and respectable, assimilating the "Higher Virtue". One must strive to obtain true happiness.

The people are a treasure generated by the "Mother/Tao". Therefore, the people (as a whole) must live freely and in peace, feeling love and joy of living. Introduce "postnatal Energy" into yourselves in order to have vivacity, valuing life and having longevity. Feel the love and feel the joy of living.

Poem seventy – six

The human body is fragile and flexible when it is born. With age it gradually becomes stiffer, and perishing, it becomes hard. Plants are also soft and fragile while growing. However, being cut, they dry up and wither.

Therefore, those who are hard and strong favor death in the same way those who are soft favor life. Strong soldiers will be defeated and stiff trees end up breaking. Thus, strong and stiff occupy the lower place, while weak and soft have a higher spot. The soft and weak ones are placed above the strong and stiff.

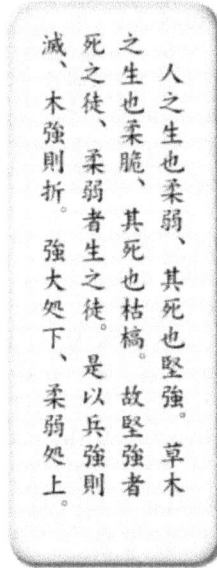

人之生也柔弱、其死也堅強。草木
之生也柔脆、其死也枯槁。故堅強者
死之徒、柔弱者生之徒。是以兵強則
滅、木強則折。強大處下、柔弱處上。

"枯" – The life of the plant ceases.

The left part of the kanji "木" >> " 米 " means Yang Energy in its upper half and Yin Energy in its lower half; "十" in the upper half of "古" represents the five Yin Energies and five Yang Energies, adding up to 10 (十). "口" >> "〇" – indicates the small universe; plants. Plants age (古) and, unable to obtain Yin-Yang Energies, they dry up, in the same way that countries with oppressive governments are defeated. Weak and flexible plants which sway with the wind survive, while the strong and stiff ones are broken and die.

Poem seventy – seven

Tao resembles the act of drawing the bowstring. One pulls down the bottom of the bow and the top rises, seeking the balance between both. So, Tao diminishes what is exceeding and completes what is missing, also seeking for balance.

天之道其猶張弓与。
高者抑之、下
者舉之。有余者損之、
不足者補之。
天之道損有余而補不足。
人之道則不
然、損不足以奉有余。
孰能有余以奉
天下。唯有道者。
是以聖人、為而不
恃、功成而不処、
其不欲見賢。

Because they maintain the balance of Yin-Yang, the people live in equality, being consolidated as a peaceful nation. However, many countries, in opposition to the laws of "Sky and Tao", adopt unnatural politics, asking high taxes of those who live with difficulty and offering liberties to those who already have plenty. Those who have too much feed their greed more and more, living a luxurious life, showing no signs of benevolence towards the people and not thinking about helping or providing for them. Only those who have assimilated Tao can take from themselves to give to those in need.

Thus, even if the Sacred Master offers his mercy or provides what is missing, he does not expect retribution. He does not boast of his acts, nor seeks fame even if he is successful in his intent. He does not desire to show his wisdom to men, only thinking in the happiness of the people through the understanding of Tao and the Virtue.

"奉" - To offer, to give, to worship

"三" – the upper stroke indicates Sky, the middle one indicates all existences, and the lower stroke indicates earth.

"人" – indicates the people. "丿" indicates Yang and "乀" indicates Yin.

The lower part of the *kanji* "奉", that is, "半", indicates "⊥", the surface of the earth, and "т" indicates the underground. Both of them together indicate this union of sky and earth.

All existences join sky and earth through Yin and Yang, making all organic things, existing on earth and underground, grow worshipping sky/God. Present yourself to the people and nourish them with Yin-Yang.

Master Lao Tzu and the Taoists say that the money necessary for a whole lifetime is limited. If there is any leftover, it should be used on behalf of society, of the people, because the state of a Sacred Master is "mercy", is giving the surplus to the people, cradled in the arms of the mother, joining sky and earth.

I have been dedicating myself to the dissemination of Qigong throughout the world according to this teaching of Tao.

186

Poem seventy – eight

In this world there is nothing softer and weaker than water; nonetheless, nothing has more power of overcoming hard and strong things than water.

Water is Yin, and there is nothing softer and weaker than it in the Yin Energy group. Weak beats strong and soft beats hard – this truth is almost universally known, but there are few who are capable of acting accordingly.

That way, the Sacred Master calls emperor the one who can take upon himself all the deplorable events that happen on the land. The one responsible for the administration of the country, who takes all responsibilities upon himself, is called sovereign.

At first sight the words of Tao might even sound contradictory, but its teachings are voices from sky.

"剛" – Strong, strong-willed

"⟨ठ⟩" of "∩" indicates the small universe.

"⊥⊿" indicates the union of Yin-Yang.

"△" indicates the mountain, as well as the bowels and intestines.

The left side of "刂" indicates Yang, and the left side, Yin.

Book of the Path and the Virtue. Yin and Yang transform and develop themselves and the great master has correctly understood the laws of nature.

"Flexible beats stiff" – it is a well-known proverb, mainly among the judokas, and has been used as a life lesson for thousands of years.

Water is soft and weak, but it breaks rock. There is nothing stronger than water. And man must always behave softly, with a humble and passive attitude (weak). However, by capturing "*Chi*" (Energy) daily and creating a sound andhealthy body, one must share with others the huge benefits one has received.

This can also be considered as an act of mercy dedicated to the people, just like water distributes nutrients to all living beings.

One can assert that "water is the master of life".

Poem seventy – nine

An intense resentment leaves traces even
when reconciliation occurs; although one
thinks or wishes to do good, there will be
times when one will be misunderstood or
will cause jealousy.

This way, the Sacred Master does not
criticize, even when people do not keep
their promises and, since the beginning,
does not take attitudes that may cause
resentment. It is simple: virtuous people
keep their promises; those who cannot
honor their commitments have no Virtue.
And Tao, not having an authoritarian or
centralizing figure which controls all, is
equal for everyone, always taking the side
of good.

無德司徹。天道無親、常与善人。

以聖人執左契而不責於人。有德司契、

和大怨必有余怨。安可以為善。是

"和" – To soften; to be friendly

"禾" – indicates that there is sky/Cosmos above the tree.

"口" – means " ᕼ ", small universe.

Like the tree "木", we receive Energy from the Cosmos through the
hypophysis. Our body, full of Energy, softens, improving the ratio of Yin/
Yang, becoming "peaceful" (和). Social coexistence naturally creates some
"resentment".

The Sacred Master advises: try not to act. Leave it to sky, God and Tao to
transform and create.

Poem eighty

In a small country with few inhabitants, even if there are people of great wisdom or practical tools and instruments, they are sometimes not used.

The people value life, which is only one, and leave everything that refers to the external world at the mercy of Sky, God and Tao; they do not think of taking even one step outside this wonderful country, and even though they have boats or wagons, they do not feel the need to go away.

Even if they have armors and weapons, they do not have contact with others nor wish to fight. These men live in a world where war and fights do not exist. They do not write nor have books. They show their intentions by talking or intertwining ropes in various ways.

They do not enjoy abundant meals nor adorn themselves with luxurious garments. They live peacefully in simple houses, helping one another, leading a happy community life.

Even if the neighboring country is so close it can be seen, even if one can hear the cackling of hens or the barking of dogs, the people do not visit the other nation until their last days.

I [Lao Tzu] consider it the ideal country. Taoists call it "Tōgenkyō" (paradise).

小国寡民、使有什伯之器而不用。
使民重死而不遠徒。雖有舟輿、無所
乗之、雖有甲兵、無所陣之。使人復
結繩而用之、甘其食、美其服、安其
居、楽其俗、隣国相望、鶏犬之声相
聞、民至老死不相往来。

"器" Recipient

"品" : indicates a recipient where everything can be put.

"大": means that such recipient unites Yin and Yang.

With the union of Yin-Yang, several recipients are created, instruments, household utensils, ceramics, etc.

桃源郷 "Tōgenkyō" (paradise)

Taoists called the ideal country "Tōgenkyō" (paradise). It means, basically, "community which lives in a peaceful world in a natural environment."

All men who love Tao and nature should build a country like this, having a long, healthy life, living close to nature, helping one another with mercy and practicing Qigong! Wouldn't that be a life "truly" worth living?

In Japan, the Ainu people lived in *tōgenkyō* (paradise), and in Brazil some Indians (native people) live in *tōgenkyō*, isolated.

The Chinese government affirms that, currently, the country is composed by 56 different peoples. However, it is possible that there is a *tōgenkyō* (some kind of isolated village, hidden in an unknown spot in the country) where people live peacefully.

Poem eighty – one

True words are not elegant nor seem triumphant; those which are spoken to seem elegant or delicate are unworthy of trust. A good man who has assimilated Tao and the virtue is not "eloquent", for eloquent or articulate people give an impression of having ulterior motives. There are few truly good people. A true wise person, even if knowing Tao and the Virtue, does not have vast knowledge; in contrast, those with vast knowledge know almost nothing about Tao and the Virtue.

The Sacred Master does not accumulate benefits or virtues upon himself; when he is asked, he explains about Tao patiently, and, by offering virtues to others, he receives gratitude, accumulating more and more of the Virtue and conquering the state of Tao. The "Path and the Virtue" of the Sacred Master only bring benefits; it transforms and creates with Yin-Yang Energies.

"老"

The *kanji* of Master Lao Tzu, known as Old Master (老子仙人) was chosen to appear last. It means someone who has accumulated years of life with vast experience and elevated virtue.

"土" :Union of sky and earth; "ノ": Energy descending into earth endlessly; "ヒ": transformation of earth/Yin into sky/Yang. By joining sky, God and Earth daily, studying Tao and accumulating vast experience, one shall become a master of many virtues.

Taoists and the Sacred Master are not eloquent, although they are excellent human beings. They are not "wise" nor possess vast knowledge, and much less seek to accumulate material goods and virtues in their own behalf. They mercifully lead the people towards Tao. The foundations of their character are simplicity and parsimony. They do not look for a great Tao all at once, advancing one step at a time. They know life is ephemeral, therefore, they live following the teachings of Tao and the Virtue.

Master *Chang Zi Yang* used to say that the ones who are eager for material goods do not realize they wither physically and spiritually and do not know where the treasure lies. However, mountain Wizards and the Sacred Masters know what lies inside the Tai Chi ball. They are cradled by the Cosmos, Tai Chi, God and Mother, achieving true happiness and living until the day they are led to the superior world. They do not pass away due to diseases, but when the prenatal and postnatal Energies are extinguished.

Everybody wishes for a serene, disease-free death. That is possible when one follows Tao and the Virtue of Master Lao Tzu and possesses the "Energy". This leads to spiritual elevation. Is that not the great goal of our lives?

6. WHAT IS QIGONG?

Qigong is a method for introducing energy. About 5000 years ago a book by the name of "黄庭経" - The book of the Yellow Emperor - was discovered inside the ruins of a castle. Taoism already existed before this book was found, but one has not found a way of proving it.

In the Yellow Emperor's Book there is an explanation of the practice of Qigong with illustrations. Reportedly, master Lao Tzu was born on February 15th, 571 B.C. at the time of the rabbit (from 5 to 7 am) and the "Book of the Path and the Virtue" was written about 2510 years ago. Since its authorship is not known for sure, the Taoists have master Lao Tzu as founder and supreme master.

Taoism teaches that God first created the Cosmos. Then he created the Yin and Yang, the stars (wind), the Sun (Yang / fire) and the moon (Yin / water). Afterwards he created the earth that received the influence of the stars of the cosmos, gradually becoming a planet with Yin-Yang balance and allowing the existence of all beings.

Nature is cyclical: it rains, water infiltrates the soil, providing Yin energy nutrients to living beings. The sun radiates heat and turns water into steam, which returns to sky. Without the wind (stars) one cannot create steam. The same happens to the human body: the upper half indicates Sky (Yang) and the lower half indicates the earth (Yin) and with the circulating current (connected to the energies of the wind and the stars) one reaches plenitude. This century, Qigong will certainly be spread worldwide, medical advances will be greater with the union of Western medicine and Taoist medicine. Therefore, Qigong is necessary as the fundamental method.

Also known as "internal development Qigong" or "Qigong method for health prevention".

1. About "Internal Qigong"

In the Cosmos there are the Yin and Yang energies that, once introduced into the body (small universe), eliminate the evil energy and provide good health and longevity, thus completing the design of Sky. "Internal Qigong" has spiritual elevation as one of its objectives.

2. Prenatal energy and postnatal energy

About Prenatal energy

The mother has Yin Energy and the father has Yang Energy. The union of these two energies generates new life.

The woman (7-year cycle) has her menstrual cycle at age 14 (2 x 7), starting to gradually lose her prenatal energy. From the age of 49 (7 x 7) until 56 or so, (7 x 8) ceases the menstrual flow. This means that the prenatal energy was reduced. From the beginning of menopause until 81 years old (9 x 9), almost all prenatal energy is lost.

After the age of 81, some women survive tenuously through nourishment (postnatal energy). Finally, with the extinction of both pre and postnatal energies, or due to disease, they end up dying.

In the case of men (8-year cycle), at the age of 16 (2 x 8) sperm becomes active and, with usage, prenatal energy is lost gradually. At 56 (7 x 8) the sperm drastically reduces. This means the decrease of prenatal energy. After the age of 64 (8 x 8), this reduction accelerates and at the age of 81 (9 x 9), as in the case of women, almost all pre and postnatal energies are lost. From this stage on, the cases of senility increase.

Western medicine has achieved wonderful progress. Even in the future, there will be an extraordinary development through research. However, even if technology continues to advance, an equipment that produces the "*Chi*" will not be created.

Taoism, through long-standing practices, has created a method of Qigong to introduce "postnatal energy". This led to the fact that many Taoists lived healthily for more than 150 years, fulfilling the skyly purpose.

About postnatal energy

In Cosmos there is the *Chi* "Energy". All existences are transformed and reborn due to the existence of *Chi*. Of all the existences, "Tao / God" allowed only Men the wisdom to introduce the energy into the body.

The *Chi* contemplates two energies: Yin and Yang. The Qigong method for introducing these energies into the body is called "Capture of postnatal energy".

Yin energy

All food comes from the earth (Yin). Vegetables, fruit, meat, fish, everything comes from the earth. The food enters the mouth and is digested by the stomach. Nutrients / "*Chi*" are stored in the Tai Chi ball and impurities are expelled through feces and urine.

Besides food, another method for introducing Yin Energy from the Earth is the practice of static and dynamic Qigong. These are methods created and developed by Taoist masters throughout 7000 years that will be explained later on.

Yang energy

In the Cosmos there are endless Yang energies. The Sun, for example, represents the Yang energy. With narrowed eyes and the tongue on the palate, at the time that goes from sunrise until about eight o'clock in the morning, look at it for three minutes. This is the best and simplest method to capture the Yang energy.

Method for introducing the Yang energy through static Qigong

One introduces it with the practice of Qigong, standing or sitting on a chair. After breathing in and focusing the energy of the Cosmos on the hypophysis, lead it calmly into the Tai Chi ball.

Method for introducing the Yang energy through dynamic Qigong

The representative method is Tai Chi Chuan. With slow and serene movements the Yang energy of the Cosmos is captured and the malignant one is expelled. However, Tai Chi Chuan requires high technique. Thus, we will present a simple and secure way to introduce Yang Energy into the body.

3. About static Qigong I - Method to obtain the "Yang Energy" from the Sun

Taoism calls "static Qigong" the method of capturing the "*Chi*" of the cosmos through the union of Man with sky and Earth in a static posture. It is an intense method which requires years of training in order to penetrate and understand the secrets of this art. The sacred masters and mountain wizards are those who have reached this stage. We shall present some Qigong exercises in a simple and effective way. Those that are not included here are explained in detail in the book "Qigong Pai Lin and Chiropractic/ Seitai with Energization", published in 2007.

Technique for introducing "Yang Energy"

All existences and all living creatures that inhabit the Earth exist due to the influences of the Sun (Yang Energy), the moon (Yin energy) and the stars.

In Cosmos there are Sky and Earth. Taoists say that our body is a small universe. In it, there are both Sky and Earth. The center of "our" Sky is the pituitary gland, which is located at the base of the brain. It is about the size of a rice grain and is connected to Sky. The Earth's central point is Hue Yin Xe, which is near the genitals. Taoists call it Yīn Qiāo. They refer to the hypophysis as Sky's gate (Yang) and to the Yīn Qiāo as Earth's door (Yin).

This technique is practiced at sunrise. Thus one will receive the Yang energy in its fullness.

The hypophysis begins to work actively, beneficially influencing the spinal cord, nerves, blood and brain cells. One rests with the *Chi*. the morning sun is a "young" one, the most appropriate because it radiates Yang energy with greater intensity.

"Morning sun" (in Taoism it is called little sun) is the rising sun. It is the scarlet sun which after five minutes or so, turns to orange in color. The best one is the scarlet-red sun.

With gratitude to Tao, I have been receiving the Yang energy through the practice of solar Qigong (internal Qigong).

Technique for introducing the Yang energy

A minute or two before sunrise, one must prepare spiritually, giving thanks and honoring Tao. Breathing should be tranquil.

1. One touches the palate slightly with the tongue, leaving the eyes narrowed.

2. One spreads one's feet roughly shoulder-width apart, turning the tips slightly to the inside.

3. One puts the palms in front of the face, turning them towards the sun. One bends the elbows about 30 degrees. Once the sun comes up, one looks in its direction, breathing in and visualizing the Yang energy entering through the eyes until it reaches the hypophysis. One breathes in for 8-12 seconds and out for around 5 seconds. This process is repeated 5 times.

4. From the 6th time on and after inhaling into the hypophysis, one exhales and visualizes the energy going down the core of the body until it reaches the Yīn Qiāo. It means that Sky and Earth have been united. The act of inhaling is longer (approximately 12 seconds) and that of exhaling is shorter.

5. From the *Yin Qiao*, one inhales again and visualizes the energy being conducted to the Tai Chi ball, located behind the navel. It means that sky and earth are united in Tai Chi. As it was before, inhaling is longer than exhaling. Proceeding the opposite way, one will eventually expel the prenatal energy. Repeat that 12 times. It is one of the secrets of Taoism.

6. People with motor difficulties or the elderly can look at the sun for only five minutes, taking care to observe the recommended times and keeping one's eyes narrowed.

7. Finalization = one puts the left palm on the navel, overlapping the right palm. One remains motionless for 12 seconds.

Before starting the exercise, it is recommended to brush the teeth and gargle.

Start after drinking water (one third of the glass).

Even on cloudy days, one should do the exercise facing the sunrise.

The best way to practice is outside, and better yet, if there is a tree nearby. When practicing indoors, open the windows wide. It is not advisable to receive the sunlight through the glass.

Depending on the location, the solar rays are very intense after at 8 am. Thus, the exercise should be done with eyes shut.

The time of the Yang energy is until 11 o'clock. Therefore, it is not recommended to practice after this time. It can harm the eyes. Practicing early in the morning is the best option.

4. Dynamic Qigong I

Tendon's exercise technique » technique to stretch the tendons.

If one practices daily, the elasticity of the tendons will improve, and then the blood flow will be better. Furthermore, it may cause the cells of nerves and muscles in our body to remain flexible, being also good for strengthening the bones and joints.

The diseases (malignant energies) arise when the circulation of blood and energy does not occur naturally.

This technique is extremely simple. Even though it is simple, human being tends not to expend the least effort to give continuity to the exercises! Both the western and the eastern medicines recommend moderate exercise. If you must choose to do only one Qigong exercise, this will certainly be the one. It is a technique to improve blood circulation throughout the body. It is advisable to practice daily.

It is also known by the name of Tai Chi Chuan in the sitting position.

[Remarks]

· The appropriate time to exercise is in the morning. The earlier, the better.

· In order to improve the blood flow, have a glass of water before starting the exercises. Warm water is recommended.

· Practice in a flat space. If practicing on hard ground, cover it with a fluffy towel.

· There is no clothing restriction as long as the clothing allows you to be at ease. It is appropriate to wear cotton socks.

· Do not practice immediately after meals. Wait at least two hours. Ideally, practice should take place before the three main meals. Slow movements are the best, ending the exercises in about 10 minutes.

· It is not advisable to practice during pregnancy.

· Practice daily.

· It is recommended for everyone, man or woman, young or old.

· With daily practice, healthy people will maintain the good health and those who have an illness will become healthy.

· Do not practice thinking about other activities other than thanking "Tao"!

How to practice

Legs stretched with the gap of a fist between the heels.

One puts the tongue on the palate. The relaxed body and the narrowed eyes must be turned towards the sun.

One puts the palms on the ground. One keeps one's back straight.

This is the initial posture.

<Picture 1>

One inhales slowly and raises one's toes. This way, the Yin energy stored in the Tai Chi ball crosses the front of the legs and is conducted to the heels.

One places one's palms beside the ears, turned towards the sun.

If the sun is not shining in the place, direct towards the window. One raises one's chin and looks up. This movement is beneficial to the cervical vertebrae, brain cells and leg muscles.

<Picture 2>

One exhales and leans one's body forward, stretching the feet toward the ground simultaneously. The Yang energy trespasses the soles of the feet and reaches the tips of the toes.

<Picture 3>

One stretches the arms respecting one's limits, as if rowing.

The Yang energy stored in the Tai Chi ball reaches the fingertips, through the outer side of the arms. At the same time the Yin energy runs through the inner side until it reaches the finger tips. As far as possible, one should not bend the knees. If one does so, the energy does not reach the fingertips in its fullness. Never exceed.

Always respect your body's limits. With daily practice, the muscles become more flexible, making the movements of the exercise easier.

One closes the hands as if holding a tennis ball.

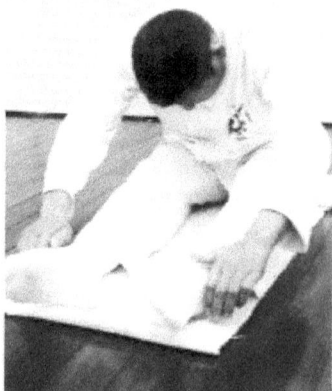

<Picture 4>

One brings the palms forward, from ankles to hips, on the side of the legs as if rowing.

This ends the first move.

The second one starts from picture number 2.

Finally, one circles the ankles 12 times from inner to outer side and vice versa. Lastly, one closes the eyes, places the palm of the left hand on the navel and overlapping it, the right palm. One concentrates the mind on the Tai Chi ball and after 12 seconds one finishes the exercise.

<Picture 5>

It was previously stated that this exercise is extremely simple. Accomplishing it or not depends solely on each person. Do not doubt its effectiveness by questioning whether it is good for your health or not to practice such a simple exercise.

It is beneficial to the spine, hips, legs and the digestive system. It also improves both blood and energy flow, favoring the brain.

If there is not any concern about capturing the "postnatal energy" during the physical activities one cannot have a long life and healthy life. That is what 7000 years of Taoist history attest.

Yin/Yang balance technique » technique for introducing the postnatal energy through Yin/Yang balance

This technique was taught by Master *Liu Pai Lin* one year before his death in 2000.

Exercise steps

Facing the sun or in front of a window, one stands up with the body in complete relaxation, feet about a fist apart and knees slightly bent.

One places the tongue on the palate, and with eyes narrowed, one feels as if in the clouds, joining sky and earth.

<Picture 1>

One takes a step forward with the left foot, leaving a space of about 40 to 50 cm (shoulder width) between one ankle and the other. One balances the body weight at the central point between the ankles. With knees slightly bent and palms alongside the hips, one initiates the movement after standing still for 5 or 6 seconds.

<Picture 2>

One slowly raises the arms to the height of the face, as if holding a ball with fingers slightly closed.

At the same time one lifts the right heel with the toes on the floor, transferring the body weight to the left foot.

<Picture 3>

One slowly takes the hands back to starting position, transferring the body weight to the right foot which must be firmly on the ground.

Simultaneously one lifts the left foot toes with the heel flat on the ground.

Do it 60 times.

<Picture 4>

One returns to position as in photo 1. Next, one does the exercise taking a step forward with the right foot. One relaxes the shoulders and keeps focused on the move.

One resumes in the same way after staying still for 5 or 6 seconds.

<Picture 5>

Taking as reference Picture 3, one slowly raises the arms face height, as if holding a ball.

One lifts the left heel, bringing the body weight to the right foot. On this occasion, feeling a pleasant tingling in the palms is a sign that the Yin and Yang energies coming from the Universe have reached the Tai Chi ball.

<Picture 6>

Taking picture 4 as reference, one slowly brings back the hands to starting position, transferring the body weight to the left foot, which must be firmly on the ground. At the same time, one raises the right toes with the heel flat on the floor.

Do it 60 times.

<Picture 7>

In order to finish the exercise, the feet should be aligned, with more or less a fist between them. This opening is required so that the Yin energy door (*Yin Qiao*) does not suffer constriction.

One places the left palm on the navel and, over it, the right palm. One remains in this position for approximately 12 seconds.

<Picture 8>

Practicing this exercise along with the stretching of the tendons will provide greater benefits. There are many reports of people who have managed to improve physical condition or heal from diseases through the technique of balance between Yin and Yang. Therefore, practice is advisable to those who have already resorted to Western medicine, acupuncture, moxibustion and have failed to improve completely.

Taoism preaches: believe in *"Chi"*, practice Qigong exercises and you will certainly have good results. This technique is useful to geriatrics, in a time when the treatment of the elderly has become a social problem. The practitioner will hardly suffer from senility. In the case of diseases in their early stage, the probability of cure is high with the regular practice of exercises.

Patients who are unable to remain standing up or who have difficulty in the legs can practice sitting. In this case, one does not lean ones back on the chair's backrest, remaining in an upright posture. Those who suffered a CVA (stroke) can practice joining hands and, as far as possible, doing the exercise without bending the elbow. One should practice several times without separating the palms. One should not forget the position of the tongue on the palate.

What is the best time to exercise?

Up to 11 a.m., when the Yang energy is more active. The earlier the better. The effects of this exercise are slower in the afternoon, when the Yin energy predominates.

How often should one practice?

The more times the better. In the beginning or until one gets used to it, approximately 60 times on each side. The idea in this case is to practice keeping track of the time and not of the number of times practiced. Begin by doing it for about 10 minutes in total. The longer the practice, the better the results. If tired, stop and rest a bit.

Wait at least two hours after meals to start the practice. The best thing to do is to establish a period of time for practicing. After 1 or 2 months one will start to feel better.

This is a Taoist secret technique that is being revealed. Have faith in the exercise and practice daily and with gratitude to Tao.

5. About static Qigong II / Xiǎo Zhou Tiān Technique (Small Universe Circulation)

In nature there is the great universe and all existences. These are the moon, the sun and the stars. Taoism conceives the human body as a small universe. The postnatal energy introduced into the body circulates and is deposited on the *Tāi Yuán Xué*, that is, the Tai Chi ball located behind the navel.

In both static and dynamic Qigong there are several techniques. At the end of every exercise, it is necessary to practice the *Xiǎo Zhou Tiān* (Circulation of the Small Universe technique) to bring back to the Tai Chi ball all the energy that has been spread throughout the body.

The basis of the body lies in the Tāi Yuán Xué/ Tai Chi ball. There is prenatal energy circulating throughout the body during practice. By introducing the postnatal energy they merge and are deposited on the Tai Chi ball.

Observe nature. Clouds are formed, rain falls, and water goes into the ground. With the sun's Yang energy warming up the Earth, the water turns into steam and goes back to sky. It is a cycle in which the water circulates endlessly. The living beings are born and transform themselves under this condition. During Xiǎo Zhou Tiān practice our body merges with nature, being able to have a long life. Constant practice preserves prenatal energy, prevents disease, and even if you are sick, if you have an active "*Chi*" you can be cured. At the end of the exercises, doing it once or twice is enough. If you practice it as a static Qigong activity, it is advisable to gradually increase from 12 times to 24, 36, 48 and 60 times.

Xiao Zhou Tiān technique in sitting posture
Small Universe circulation

Xiǎo Zhōu Tiān⌋ - Zhòn Gyào Xué – **The vital Points**

1. *Bǎi Huì* (Top of the head)

2. Qí (Navel)

3. *Yīn Qiāo* (Yin energy input)

4. *Wěi Lǘi*

5. *Xiān Gū*

6. *Mìng Mén* (Point between the kidneys)

7. *Xìn Qiào* (Quadruplet body)

8. *Jī Tái* (Pineal Gland)

9. *Líng Tái* (Third Ventricle)

10. *Rǔ Bǔ* (Hypophysis)

11. *Yuán Shén* (Central Point – Yang Energy)

12. *Tāi Yuán Xué* (Tai Chi ball) or *Tai Chi Qiú*

13. *Yìn Táng* (between the eyebrows)

Practice steps

(1) One sits on a chair in upright posture without leaning on the chair's backrest but loosely at the same time. The feet should be firmly on the ground, with the tips facing slightly inwards. The distance between the knees must be the exact shoulder length.

(2) Make Bǎi Huì (point at the top of the head) and Yīn Qiāo (Yin energy input) form a straight line.

(3) All exercises are done with the tongue touching the palate. Even this Xiǎo Zhou Tiān technique (Small Universe circulation) is no exception. If one does not touch the palate with the tongue, the union between sky and earth will not occur.

(4) Join your left hand's thumb and middle finger together and place your right thumb on the circle formed. "Embrace "the left hand with the four fingers of the right one. (Yin embraces Yang), placing both hands slightly below the navel.

(5) Keep your eyes closed and stay in a posture in which you feel as if Bǎi Huì were being pulled upward. Visualize the "union of sky, man and earth."

(6) Visualize several stars and remain in this state for 1 or 2 minutes.

(7) Inhale slowly (minimum of 12 s) and imagine that the energy is entering the space between the eyebrows (Yin Tan point) and the top of the head (Bǎi Huì point), being led into the Ling Tai. Hold your breath for 3 seconds

(8) Exhale calmly, visualizing that the energy descends and goes through the hypophysis, tongue, throat, chest, navel and goes into the Yīn Qiāo. Exhale for less time than the time of inhalation. **This is a very important detail.**

212

(9) After 3 seconds, inhale calmly, visualizing that the energy follows the path *Xiān Gū* (5) to the lumbar vertebra → thoracic vertebrae→ cervical vertebrae (always at the outer side of the vertebrae). Next, continue inhaling *Xīn Chiào* wise (7) → *Jī Tái* (8) → *Líng Tái* (9). The slower, the better.

(10) After stopping for 3-5 seconds at *Líng Tái*, swallow the saliva (even if there is almost nothing) and exhale slowly , leading the "Energy" to *Rŭ Bŭ* (hypophysis- 10) → *Yuán Shén* (center point of the chest - 11) , and finally the central point of *Tāi Yuán Xué* (Tai Chi ball - 12).

When finished, breathe naturally, wait a few seconds and repeat the practice. You can do it a minimum of 7 and a maximum of 60 times.

The important thing is to inhale longer and exhale in less time, in order to preserve the prenatal energy. It is recommended to inhale slowly for 12 seconds or more and exhale in less time. Taoists and sacred masters can inhale for up to one minute.

The best way practice is facing north. There is a legend among Taoists that indicates the direction of the Ursa Major constellation as that which holds the most active energy. There is no need, however, to worry much about practicing towards that direction.

The exercise can be done outdoors or indoors. If outdoors, practicing in the morning in a quiet place close to trees and sitting opposite to the sun. In the morning, trees release the "energies"; but in the afternoon, they steal it by absorption. It is therefore not recommended to practice in the afternoon near the trees.

All exercises should be practiced after oral hygiene, that is, after brushing your teeth or gargling. When one gets up in the morning the mouth is full of malign energies. Drink water, approximately one third of a glass. If you're thirsty, it's okay to have a glass of water. This is the water that shall become part of the postnatal energy.

It is almost impossible to become a Taoist or sacred master without going through this *Xiau Zhou* Tian exercise (Small Universe circulation). It holds the wisdom of the Taoists. Practice it daily with respect and gratitude.

Four internal Qigong techniques were presented in the hopes that all of them might be practiced for about two hours on a daily basis. That way, one can have a comfortable life, with longevity and health.

Taoist masters, sacred Masters, Mountain Wizards, all rise between 3 and 4 o'clock in the morning and dedicate themselves to internal Qigong exercises until around 11 am; they have a long, healthy life and when the time of going into the spiritual world comes, their bodies remain sound while the Yang energy is extinguished (spirit). They go to Sky led by God after there is a wake and their bodies (Yin energy) are buried in the presence of family members and Taoist disciples.

Master Lao Tzu made several references to the "mercy." It is recommended, therefore, to devote oneself to the study of the "Path and the Virtue", as well as to the static Qigong, in order to receive the maternal mercy (cosmos). Such is mercy, men joining sky and earth, capturing the post-natal energy.

In order to achieve it, one of the most appropriate exercises is *Xiau Zhou* Tian (Small Universe circulation).

Difference between "周" and "週"

The *kanji* 周 is used for personal names, those of provinces etc. But 周 has the sense of "a spin around something." Thus, the Taoists use *kanji* 周 when it comes to the Small Universe circulation technique.

8. EXTERNAL QIGONG INSTRUCTION MANUAL

External Qigong is a method in which the patient is treated by eliminating the maleficent energy (disease) through the introduction of the external energy of the cosmos, thus complementing the vital "Energy". Disease is caused by stagnation of the blood's energy inside the internal organs.

The Qigong practitioner stimulates the patient's prenatal energy through external Qigong. The patient receives this energy stimulation through the 8 meridians and thus, health improvement is obtained.

When a person is sick, the maleficent energy and the prenatal energy engage in a fight. Disease (maleficent energy) is overcome when external energy is transmitted by the Qigong practitioner and reinforces the patient's prenatal energy.

According to Oriental medicine, in the Cosmos lies the energy of the 5 elements (fire, earth, metal, water and wood) and of the 5 colors (red, yellow, white, black and blue), which are connected to the five fingers of the hands, through which the "Energies" radiate. Any treatment should be done with the understanding of that fact.

Qigong has gradually been spread worldwide and it is believed that it will become part of the treatment of diseases, with the development of researches regarding its benefits.

In China, it already has official recognition from the Ministry of Health, and there is a Therapy through Qigong Department, contributing to the healing of many sick people.

For effective treatment through external Qigong, the therapist must have a secure knowledge of Taoism, Oriental Medicine and Internal Qigong. If one applies the external Qigong treatment without practicing internal Qigong, one will certainly lose one's own prenatal energy and end up drastically shortening one's life.

The ideal time for treatment is until 11 am, when nature creates and provides numerous energies. With the union of sky - therapist - patient – Earth, postnatal energy is introduced, strengthening the body and eliminating maleficent energy (disease). Nature (Tao/ God) will help in the therapeutic Qigong treatment.

A Qigong treatment session should last approximately 20 minutes. Therefore, on that day, it is necessary for the therapist to engage 20-30 minutes longer in internal Qigong exercises in the morning, for each patient that will be treated.

If he dominates the practice, the practitioner may apply it for a group of 2-5 people in one session. The therapist who wants to devote himself to this technique should study the chapter on "Internal Qigong" profoundly, as well as practice the exercises recommended there.

For the treatment, the external energy (Yin – Yang energy) is concentrated at the fingertips and at the center of the palms. It is necessary to apply it for about 20 minutes and, if applying it a second time to the same patient, it can be done in less time, for when the body receives the *Chi*, it activates its natural healing ability.

During treatment, there may be a movement of legs or hands due to improved blood and energy circulation. However, the therapist must always be alert to reactions from the patient and stop a session if they feel uncomfortable.

Through *Chi* (Energy), both internal and external Qigong aim to increase the ability of an individual to prevent disease and improve their health and that of others. If Qigong therapists happen to attain a higher stage, their treatments will increasingly assist in the recovery and healing of sick people.

The XXI century's best therapy will arise when there is unity between eastern and western medicine.

216

Preventive medicine and treatment - more efficient care

All diseases that affect human beings can be treated, but in the initial stage, the probability of cure is greater. Chronic problems are more difficult. A chronic patient can be treated and improve, but the chances of cure are lower.

[Warning]

It is recommended not to treat the elderly who have the area from the palms to the elbows too cold. They have very little *"Chi"* (energy), being difficult to be cured and they may actually be on the verge of death.

Before starting treatment through Qigong techniques, check the patient's pulse. Those with less than 50 heartbeats are in critical condition and so are those who have it high, too.

Treatment should be discontinued if the patient's heartbeat increases and he feels bad. The procedure should be the same if the pulse slows down.

External Qigong Shioda style can only benefit the patient and has no contraindication. However, some lines of external Qigong have patients undergoing more intense treatments, which can cause serious problems. Thus, it is important to be prevented.

The practice of external Qigong is not recommended to extremely ill patients such as those suffering from terminal cancer.

On some occasions during the treatment of external Qigong, the patient may experience more pain and not achieve the expected results.

The therapist must then decide carefully whether to continue the treatment or stop it. In most cases, the continuity promotes a progressive improvement in the patient's condition.

In patients who have experienced a CVA (stroke) or a heart attack, even if they feel a little pain, if the pulse is normal, the practitioner can proceed with the treatment.

The application of external Qigong is not suitable for those who suffer from mental illness and schizophrenia.

Those who take painkillers do not have much sensitivity to *Chi*.

It is not suitable for those who tire easily or when the person does not feel right.

To those who take medicine, treatment is recommended when the medicine is not working.

One should suspend the treatment when there is thunder, for thunders block the energy. One could say the same about the practice of internal Qigong.

External Qigong is not appropriate in a place where there are many sick patients or in hospital rooms, as these environments are infested with maleficent energies.

It should not be applied to individuals under the influence of alcohol.

Both external and internal Qigong are not recommended when there is fog, for it is a sign that the maleficent energy has emerged.

The therapist must practice internal Qigong for a few minutes before initiating a consultation. It is recommended to do the Small Universe circulation exercise.

Apply the treatment believing in the cure, in a relaxed way, thinking about nothing, in a state of *"Mu"*.

It is difficult to determine how many sessions can heal. Ideally 4 or 5 at least, not too many days apart. More serious diseases require longer treatment.

If one can make the patient learn and practice the internal Qigong exercises at home, the results will be better. Just follow the techniques presented in this book.

In the current scenario, the treatment with external Chi Kung is performed with each therapist adapting it to their own style.

This book seeks to systematize the treatments through external Qigong, whose basis I have received from four great Qigong masters: *Liu Pai Lin*, Yoshitsugu Hayashi, Zhāng Yǔ and acupuncturist Liu Chih Ming.

Master Liu Pai Lin
11th. Master of Lóng Mén School

Master Yoshitsugu Hayashi
12th Master of Lóng Mén School

Right: Master Zhāng Yǔ
Left: author 12th - Lóng Mén School

Right: autor
Left: Master Liu Chih Ming

Master Yoshitsugu Hayashi, Master Liu Chih Ming and Master Kenichi Shioda are currently the only successors of the 12th Taoist Lóng Mén (Dragon Gate) lineage.

A. External Qigong treatment in sitting posture

Before the consultation, perform the internal Qigong technique. Ask the patient questions about their health.

1. Check the pulse.

2. Examine the patient's tongue. If it is dark red in color, the application of external Qigong is not recommended.

3. The patient should sit in a chair, keep their back straight and feet flat on the floor, shoulder-width spread. The palms should be on the knees, facing upward.

4. They are asked to close their eyes and keep the tongue on the palate.

220

» (1) Prayer

Pray for Tao and for a guiding spirit asking
for their protection: "Eliminate the malignant
energy (disease) from this patient "- repeat the
phrase three times. The left palm = Yang and the
right palm = Yin unite just below the nose.

In order to preserve his vital energy during
treatment, the therapist must keep the tongue
away from the palate.

» (2) Purification

Approach the patient (around 20 cm) and remove
the negative energy using the back of the hands,
as if you were cleaning them from head to toe.
To expel all maleficent energies of the patient,
both palms and all fingers are used. Move the
fingertips away around 20 cm from the patient's
body. Repeat the purification move for 20 to
30 seconds.

» (3) Circulation of Energy

Having the patient›s Tai Chi ball and navel as
central spot, rotate the palms clockwise, making
the prenatal energy circulate throughout the
whole body, making the therapist's palms turn
clockwise. Take 20 to 30 seconds to do this
procedure.

» (4) Chi through the eyes

With the middle and index fingers together and at a distance of 2 to 3 cm, the therapist transmits the *Chi* through the patient's eyes. He does not touch the eyes, but moves the fingers as if pushing the energy into them for 1 to 2 minutes.

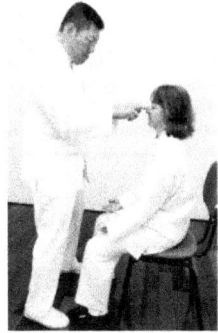

» (5) Chi in the Tai Chi ball and Min Men (point between the kidneys)

The *Chi* is simultaneously introduced into the Tai Chi ball and into the Min Men, placing the right palm 2, 3 cm from the Tai Chi ball (navel), and the left palm 2, 3 cm from the Min Men (point between the kidneys at the 12th thoracic vertebra's height). For 1 to 2 minutes transmit the energy as if touching the Tai Chi ball. The time required is from 1 to 2 minutes.

» (6) *Xiǎo Zhou Tiān* (Small Universe Circulation).

With the right palm, apply the *Chi* following the sequece: *Líng Tái* – down – hypophysis – throat – chest – navel - *Yīn Qiāo* – up – sacrum bone - lumbar vertebrae – thoracic vertebrae - cervical vertebrae - *Líng Tái* – down – hypophysis – throat – chest – navel (Tai Chi Ball).

In the first point, transmit the Energy for approximately 10 seconds. It takes about 1 minute to complete all the *Xiǎo Zhou Tiān* movements.

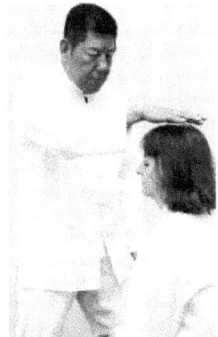

» (7) Chi through *Băi Huì* (top of the head)

With your left hand on top of your right hand 2 to 3 cm above the *Băi Huì* point, lead the energy slowly, in a straight line, moving from the *Yuán Shén* point (11) to the Tai Chi Ball's center. Apply this step for 1 minute.

» (8) Chi in the *Rŭ Bŭ* (hypophysis) and *Xìn Chiào*

Place the right palm's center at a distance of 2 or 3 cm from the point between the eyes. The left palm should be behind the head 2 or 3 cm from the *Xìn Chiào* point. Apply the *Chi* in the *Rŭ Bŭ* and in the *Xìn Chiào* simultaneously, for approximately one minute.

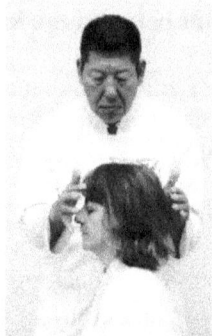

» (9) Chi in the *Yuán Shén* point

Energize the *Yuán Shén* point (center of the chest) for 1 minute with the right palm's center positioned 2 to 3 cm from the patient and the left palm's center positioned on the back, at the same height, next to the 7th. Thoracic vertebra.

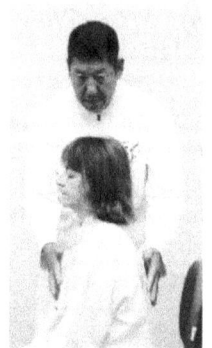

Yuán Shén is the Yang Energy's central point.

» (10) Chi on the palms of the hands

On the palm of the hand are represented all the human being's organs. Applying the *Chi* on the hands benefits the whole body.

In the patient's right palm, place both the palms and lead the energy for approximately one minute.

Then apply in the left hand.

» (11) Chi in the pain or disease points

With one or both palms overlapping, lead the energy into the area where the patient feels discomfort or pain, during 2 to 3 minutes. If one has a stomach or spleen problem, for example, concentrate the *Chi* at these points. The procedure is the same for any illness.

» (12) The Chi through the eyes

Again, the therapist transmits the *Chi* through the patient's eyes with the middle and index fingers together at a distance of 2 to 3 cm. Move the fingers for 1 to 2 minutes, as if pushing the energy into the eyes. At the bottom of the point between the eyes is located the *Rǔ Bǔ*. Leading the *Chi* through his point, which has deep relation with the spine, is beneficial to the whole body.

» (13) Chi in the pain or diseases points

Again, come back to the area where the patient feels discomfort or pain and lead the energy with one or both palms overlapping during 2 to 3 minutes. According to the five elements theory, the spleen and the stomach are "sons" of the heart and small intestine. Thus, leading the energy into them will strengthen the spleen and the stomach.

» (14) Finalization (1)

The energy which has been spread through the patient's body should return to the navel's point (Tai Chi Ball). With the right palm, follow the sequence: right leg - navel, left leg - navel, right arm - navel, left arm - navel and from top of the head to the navel. The procedure takes approximately one minute.

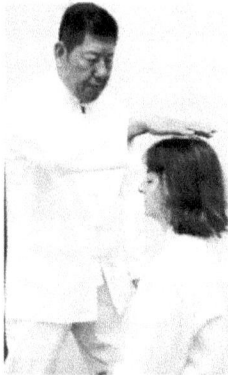

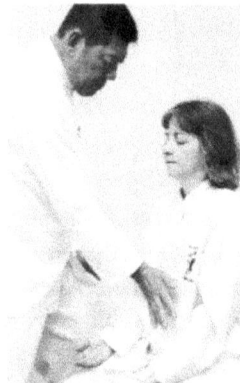

» (14) Finalization (2)

At the end, using the index and middle fingers, touch the patient's shoulders lightly and ask them to open their eyes calmly.

» (15) Detailed record of the procedures' results in a medical record

Most commons reports:

The patient visualized colors.

Reason: One sees the 5 colors with the introduction of *Chi* from the Cosmos. White and blue are common.

The patient felt a warmth in the body and sweated a little.

Reason: The introduction of *Chi* from the Cosmos eliminates the negative Energies through sweat.

Tearing up

Reason: The *Chi* introduced by the therapist causes the elimination of the negative through the tears. It is a sign that mainly the liver's maleficent Energy was expelled.

Involuntary movement of hands and feet

Reason: The movement happens because the circulation of *Chi* is obstructed and the patient's own body tries to clear the passage. Since this is a good sign, the therapist should continue with the procedure.

The patient felt comfortable when they opened their eyes after the treatment.

Reason: the patient's prenatal energy circulates in the External Qigong treatment, therefore, the maleficent Energy is eliminated, resulting in *Chi's* natural flow, which is very good.

(16) Advice and warnings to the patient

Instruct the patient about the benefits of practicing "Internal Qigong" presented in this book. The ideal would be to practice all the exercises. Indicate the ones that are most appropriate to each patient's needs.

Teach the *Xiau Zhou Tian* exercise posture (Small Universe Circulation) to the patient. Many times, due to putting the tongue against the palate and concentrating on the Tai Chi Ball, the results appear in a short time, providing help in therapeutic treatments.

Guide them about daily habits.

If it is possible, also guide them about their eating habits.

The use of herbs and homeopathic medicines is also beneficial.

There should be the union of the body, soul and nature, in other words, "Sky/therapist and patient/earth." It is the best treatment that Tao teaches us.

External Qigong treatment, in the lying down position

The patient should lie down (abdomen facing up), with arms extended along the body and the palms turned upwards. Between the feet there should be an opening of about a fist. If the feet are closed, the Yin Energy doesn't reach the upper part of the body, and the same happens if the feet are too far apart. If the patient feels more comfortable they can lie on a pillow. Before starting the treatment, ask the patient to keep their eyes closed (without sleeping) and the tongue on the palate. Ask them not to be afraid if they see colors, lights or movements.

Since the initial steps are similar to the External Qigong treatment, in sitting posture, we will not include them here.

(1) Chi in the Líng *Tái* for the union with the *Yīn Qi*āo

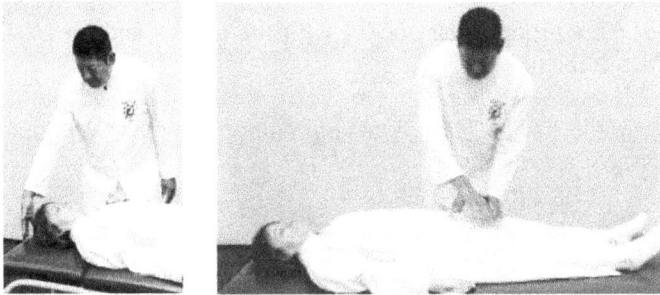

It's important to be relaxed.

Place the right palm at a distance of 2 or 3 cm away from the patient's *Băi Huì* point (top of the head). Look mentally to the *Líng Tái*. After approximately 12 seconds, come down slowly to the *Rŭ Bŭ* (hypophysis), throat, chest, navel until the *Yīn Qiāo. Líng Tái* means to unite Sky and the Sun, as well as the *Yīn Qiāo,* the Earth and Yin- Yang. Do this movement twice, for approximately 2 minutes. This treatment can be done with one or both palms.

(2) Chi in the Líng Tái and Rǔ Bǔ

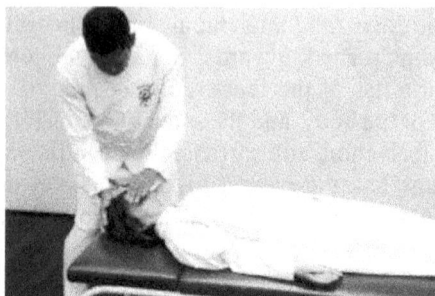

Place the center of the right palm at a distance of 2 or 3 cm away from the *Bǎi Huì*, then introduce the *Chi* into the **Líng Tái** (between the eyebrows).

At the same time, place the left palm on the point that is between the patient's eyes, 2 to 3 cm away, and introduce the *Chi* into the *Rǔ Bǔ*.

The *Líng Tái* is in deep relation with the síne; the *Rǔ Bǔ* with the spinal cord; the *Xìn Chiào* (quadruplet body) with the nerves and the *Jī Tái* (pineal gland) with the blood.

Introduce the *Chi* on these four vital points, from 1 to 2 minutes. This is one of Tao's secrets.

Important vital points

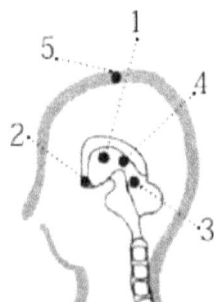

1. Líng Tái;

2. Rǔ Bǔ;

3. Xìn Qiào;

4. Jī Tái

5. Bǎi Huì

(3) The Chi in the Yuán Shén point

Between the nipples there is a point known by the Taoists as *Yuán Shén*.It has the approximate size of a baby heart or the size of a circle formed by the thumb and middle finger. Place the palms overlapping, 2 to 3 cm away from the *Yuán Shén* point, for 1 or 2 minutes.

The *Yuán Shén* point is very important because it's the central part of the Yang Energy (source, base).

When a human being passes away, this point closes. It isn't recommended to wear clothes that show this point. It must be protected.

(4) The Chi in the Tai Chi Ball

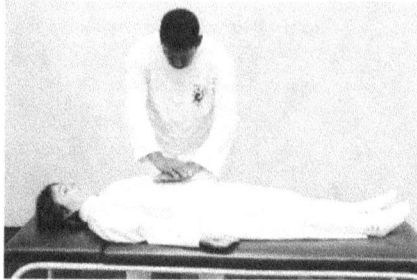

Keep your right hand on top of your left hand and place either 2 or 3 cm away from the navel.

Look mentally to the patient's Tai Chi Ball, putting the *Chi* in this point.

The sick people's Yin and Yang Energies are unbalanced, especially the "Yang Energy". In this case, it's necessary to introduce the *Chi* steadily for 1 or 2 minutes.

(5) The Chi through the soles of the feet

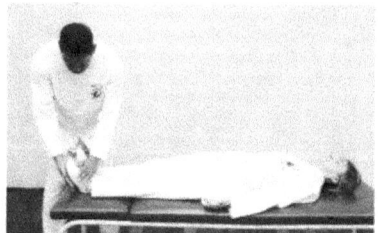

With the right palm placed on the right foot, 3-4 cm from the *Yuán Shén* point (located on the sole) and the left palm parallel to the same point on the upper part of the foot, lead the energy as if massaging the patient's foot with the *Chi*, for 2 to 3 minutes.

After about 30 seconds, the therapist should lead, consciously (intention), the *Chi* towards the Tai Chi Ball (navel) of the patient.

Next, from the sole, lead the *Chi* to the diseased part of the patient.

Contract the palms and fingers slightly, around 2 to 3 cm. Repeat the procedure on the left foot, for 2 to 3 minutes.

(6) Chi on the palms of the hands

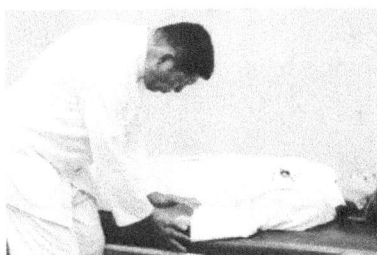

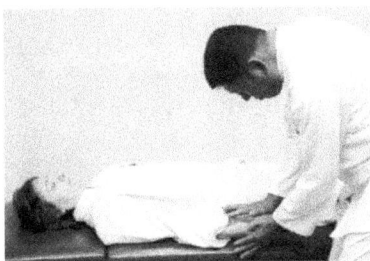

On the patient's right hand, place both the palms (one over the center of the palm and the other parallel to the first, in the back) at a distance of 3 to 4 cm. The *Chi* is introduced by imagining its radiation through the fingertips and palms, as if you were massaging the patient's hand. After 30 seconds, make the *Chi* flow to the diseased part of the patient. For example, if you are doing this on the heart, stay focused in this point, and make the *Chi* flow in this direction for 1 to 2 minutes. Repeat the procedure on the left hand for 1 to 2 minutes.

When the therapist is moving around the patient, he must always move clockwise in order to complement the *Chi*. Circulating in the counterclockwise direction causes the loss of *Chi*. Even the acupuncturist, massage therapist or another therapist should do the same.

One mustn't forget the Taoist teachings.

(7) Chi in the pain or disease points

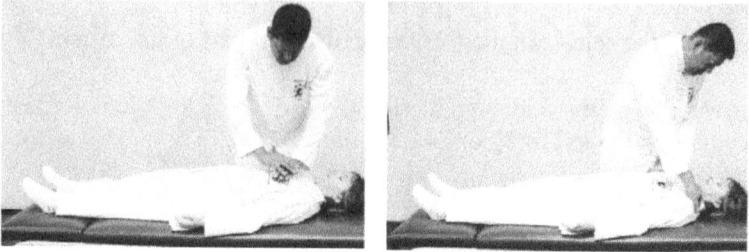

If a patient has heart problems, the therapist should position his palms overlapping at a distance of 4-5 cm from the patient, and visualizing the heart, lead the *Chi* as if he were massaging it lightly. After 2 minutes, check the pulse. If it is normal, continue the procedure adding up to four minutes.

(8) Introduce the *Chi* again in the *Líng Tái*, Rǔ Bǔ, *Yuán Shén,* feet and palms. (Approximately 2 minutes).

(9) Introduce the *Chi*, again, in the painful or diseased points.

(10) For finalization, treatment results, advice and warnings to the patient, follow the same procedures of the External Qigong treatment in sitting posture. Because it's a very deep Taoist Qigong technique, it may not be understood by everyone. However, experience shows that the results obtained by these techniques are excellent. The therapist should have faith in the *Chi* and Tao, capturing enough postnatal Energy and dedicating himself to the treatment in a state of "Mu" (void).

The ideogram of real medicine (藥) has the meaning of: the left side of the upper part ┿ represents the Yin, the right side ┿ represents the Yang, and the middle strokes represent the 白 (white), which accepts the other 4 colors (yellow, blue, red and black), becoming 5 colors (*Chi*, 5 elements of Yin-Yang). The strokes on the sides of 白■ ■, were written 幺 幺 that is, the *kanji* was the way we see beside . 幺 » ○ – the upper part represents Sky,

Yang, the upper part of the human body, and the lower part represents earth, Yin, and the and lower part of the human body. In addition, "木" exists on the earth. They are herbs, leaves, trunk, bark, roots and fruit that becomes medicine (薬).

薬

Therefore, it is possible to understand how much the *"Chi"* and the "medicine" are important.

I hope this bilingual book is the initial step to the dissemination of these teachings, and that its constant translation into other languages reaches and benefits many people around the world. I also intend to disseminate this knowledge through lectures in several countries.

"Distribute love without expecting retribution".

"Distribute love for the maintenance of the health of all humanity, for the world peace!"

9. Teachings of Master Lao Tzu

Human beings think they are superior to other animals. However, common individuals are not so different from animals: they eat food, have sexual relations, fight, sleep… But the practice of static Qigong is what elevates the spirit and may make us different from animals.

Master Lao Tzu had "Sky" and "Earth" as his masters. When we practice Qigong, these masters will teach us.

These are some of master Lao Tzu's sayings:

"A heart that holds love and mercy."

"Do not think of becoming the best in society or among the Taoists, but think about helping other people so that they become the best."

"Spare things. If there are leftovers, share among those who are in a difficult situation. My happiness is to see other people in a better situation. If you have Taoist feelings you may have a long life at the mercy of the Supreme One."

In the path of life, one shall not reach the peak of the mountain. Face life taking one step at a time, always looking forward. If one reaches the peak, the following step is only to roll down the mountain.

The one who guides his followers must not expose himself. For instance, a king. He makes the prime minister evident by praising him in public. If the prime minister makes a mistake, the king does not reprehend him in public so that he notices his own mistake through the teachings of Tao and the Virtue.

Stop being dominated by rivalry, because you will lose the prenatal energy and shorten your life. Live like Nature.

After the forties, men usually start to worry about family, work and appearance. However, the most important is to worry about health and internal condition. The solution is the introduction of *Chi* and the teachings about Tao.

Those who have a high social status (Yang/Sky) shall take care of those who have lower social status (Yin/Earth). An ideal nation is built with the union of "Yang/Sky" and "Yin/Earth".

Selfish individuals who only think about their own happiness shall lose prenatal energy and will not be able to live in plenitude. Master Lao Tzu teaches: "Think about what you can do for other people".

Taoism preaches that the soul (Yang) does not die, even if the body (Yin) does. An individual is born by the union of body - Yin and spirit - Yang. When a person dies, the body goes into the ground and the soul returns to sky. The spirits remain. Even now, they are communicating with us. They will do so forever.

Life is the most precious gift in this world. "In order to have a long life, the only way is through Tao, the Virtue and Qigong".

10. Message of Master Liu Pai Lin

Will the reading of "The Book of the Path and the Virtue" be enough to transmit all its meaning in an understandable way?

I believe there are no lies or mistakes in the teachings of the Path and the Virtue, since Tao is about the teachings of nature, and in a way, God is Nature. Therefore, the teachings of Tao are the teachings of "God".

Be grateful for the teachings (inside the *Tao Te Ching*) because even though Lao Tzu does not have a physical body anymore, his soul is alive and communicates through his Taoist successor *Yang Xiàn Tzu* (the author).

I would like everyone to learn the technique of "introduction of post-natal energy". The Qigong techniques are secrets transmitted orally only to those who have respect for Tao. My wish is just to make the "The Book of the Path and the Virtue" public, as well as the Qigong techniques, for the good of humankind.

There are two mothers. One is the mother who gave birth to us. The other is the Cosmos. Feel embraced by the "Mother". Feel supported by her and, for those who follow the teachings of Tao with conviction and attempt to obtain the "post-natal Energy", the "Mother" certainly will offer her true love.

By proceeding this way, you shall obtain the spiritual elevation and achieve true happiness.

About the author:

Kenichi Shioda

Yang *Xiàn Tzu*

12th successor of *Lón Mén* Taoist School.

Tiān Xiàn Tzu

6th successor of *Jīn Shān* Taoist School

15th successor of *Kún Lún* Taoist School

Successor of *Qīng Chéng, Fú Qiū*, and *Tiān Shān* schools

Kenichi Shioda was born in 1947 in the city of Yokohama, Kanagawa province, Japan. He has immigrated to Brazil in 1974, living permanently in the city of São Paulo.

His master in Taoist Qigong was Liu Pai Lin. He received lessons of external Qigong (therapeutic Qigong) and Chiropractic from Master Yoshitsugu Hayashi. He was granted an official degree as a Tai Chi Chuan master (Liu Pai Lin style), as well as Bāguàzhǎng master (Pa Kua Tsam style).

He was president of the Shioda Institute, located in the city of São Paulo, Brazil.

In 1993, he was decorated by the Brazilian government with the Professor Hideyo Noguchi Collar, and in 1994 with the Grã-Cruz Medal.

Ken'ichi Shioda presented lectures and courses at São Paulo University (USP), Federal University of Paraíba, Tokyo Kogyo University (Japan), Federal University of Dakar (Senegal), Federal University of Cape Verde (Africa), and Consulate-General of Japan, Uruguay.

He is the author of "Chi Kung Pai Lin and Chiropractic/Seitai with Energization" (Paulo's Graphic Press), along with Yoshitsugu Hayashi. The book was published in 2007.